THEORY AND PRACTICE OF TEACHING

THEORY AND PRACTICE OF TEACHING

Edward Thring

General Books

www.General-Books.net

Publication Data:

Title: Theory and Practice of Teaching
Author: Edward Thring
Reprinted: 2010, General Books, Memphis, Tennessee, USA
Publisher: University press
Publication date: 1894
Subjects: Teaching
Education / General
Education / Aims Objectives
Education / Teaching Methods Materials / General
Education / Philosophy Social Aspects
History / General
BISAC subject codes: EDU000000, EDU003000, EDU029000, EDU040000, HIS000000

How We Made This Book for You
We made this book exclusively for you using patented Print on Demand technology.
First we scanned the original rare book using a robot which automatically flipped and photographed each page.
We automated the typing, proof reading and design of this book using Optical Character Recognition (OCR) software on the scanned copy. That let us keep your cost as low as possible.
If a book is very old, worn and the type is faded, this can result in numerous typos or missing text. This is also why our books don't have illustrations; the OCR software can't distinguish between an illustration and a smudge.
We understand how annoying typos, missing text or illustrations, foot notes in the text or an index that doesn't work, can be. That's why we provide a free digital copy of most books exactly as they were originally published. You can also use this PDF edition to read the book on the go. Simply go to our website (www.general-books.net) to check availability. And we provide a free trial membership in our book club so you can get free copies of other editions or related books.
OCR is not a perfect solution but we feel it's more important to make books available for a low price than not at all. So we warn readers on our website and in the descriptions we provide to book sellers that our books don't have illustrations and may have numerous typos or missing text. We also provide excerpts from books to book sellers and on our website so you can preview the quality of the book before buying it.
If you would prefer that we manually type, proof read and design your book so that it's perfect, simply contact us for the cost. Since many of our books only sell one or two copies, we have to split the production costs between those one or two buyers.

Frequently Asked Questions

Why are there so many typos in my paperback?
We created your book using OCR software that includes an automated spell check. Our OCR software is 99 percent accurate if the book is in good condition. Therefore, we try to get several copies of a book to get the best possible accuracy (which is very difficult for rare books more than a hundred years old). However, with up to 3,500 characters per page, even one percent is an annoying number of typos. We would really like to manually proof read and correct the typos. But since many of our books only sell a couple of copies that could add hundreds of dollars to the cover price. And nobody wants to pay that. If you need to see the original text, please check our website for a downloadable copy.

Why is the index and table of contents missing (or not working) from my paperback?
After we re-typeset and designed your book, the page numbers change so the old index and table of contents no longer work. Therefore, we usually remove them. We dislike publishing books without indexes and contents as much as you dislike buying them. But many of our books only sell a couple of copies. So manually creating a new index and table of contents could add more than a hundred dollars to the cover price. And nobody wants to pay that. If you need to see the original index, please check our website for a downloadable copy.

Why are illustrations missing from my paperback?
We created your book using OCR software. Our OCR software can't distinguish between an illustration and a smudge or library stamp so it ignores everything except type. We would really like to manually scan and add the illustrations. But many of our books only sell a couple of copies so that could add more than a hundred dollars to the cover price. And nobody wants to pay that. If you need to see the original illustrations, please check our website for a downloadable copy.

Why is text missing from my paperback?
We created your book using a robot who turned and photographed each page. Our robot is 99 percent accurate. But sometimes two pages stick together. And sometimes a page may even be missing from our copy of the book. We would really like to manually scan each page. But many of our books only sell a couple of copies so that could add more than a hundred dollars to the cover price. And nobody wants to pay that. If you would like to check the original book for the missing text, please check our website for a downloadable copy.

1

THEORY AND PRACTICE OF TEACHING

PREFACE TO THE FIRST EDITION.

IT is ill protesting too much. Many good resolutions of silence made and confirmed during thirty years of school-work, as every hope of a public character which brightened the early days was destroyed, have been broken by the appearance of this book. Success only strengthened the conviction that it was useless to speak; and yet when the conviction seemed strongest some folly has swept it away. Or is it instinct, like the prescient idiotcy of the butterfly, that lays its eggs on cabbage leaf, or nettle, forced by a blind impulse to thwart its own experience, and deposit part of its life where no sign warrants an idea that it will be allowed to live? Perhaps a strong belief that anything, which has a touch of true life in it, will live somewhere or other is at the bottom of it all, however overlaid by chiller wisdom. So this bit of life goes forth. And if it does any work or worker good, cheers, or helps a single toiling fellow-creature, the writer will have had his reward. It may be that another hand and heart may take this up, enrich it with wealth of his own, fill it full of prevailing power, and send it on, a higher creation, in a fortunate hour, to a happier end.

The School House, Uppingham,
May, 1883.

PREFACE TO THE SECOND EDITION.

HE, who from whatever motive appears for a lost cause, may be well pleased at obtaining a hearing; and need not wonder if the toleration granted him be somewhat due to an unconsciousness of the meaning of his statements. If a nation has in practice decided against teaching, it is likely that they will take the word in their own sense and refuse to admit a different interpretation of it. Hence the uselessness of speaking on the subject. But the hope that a workers words might cheer and help fellow-workers has been fully verified. So the author, joining hands with English-speaking brethren in far distant lands, sends out this second edition cheered and strengthened himself by having cheered and strengthened others; certain now that there are seeds of life in it, which touch other lives, even as they came out of his own life first.

The School House, Uppingham,
May, 1885.

PREFACE TO THE THIRD EDITION.

TV T OTHING is so wonderful in modern times as the-marvellous communion and circulation of life. Thought and feeling in perpetual currents of living intercourse, literature, politics, books, visibly and invisibly, ebb and flow over the whole earth. Like the rain, they fall everywhere; like water, they find their own level, and if checked in one place reappear as fountains in another. Rock and clay are omnipotent to dam them back from themselves, by an omnipotence, which sends them as rivulets with fertilising power elsewhere. This little book put forth with many misgivings as a bit of life, yet with some confidence that what came from life would touch the lives of others, has not belied that hope. Its

CHAPTER I.

THE THEORY OF TEACHING.

Olla Podrida.

Some people have thought that vast changes demand something more definite to justify them than a vast difficulty; and sympathise with the hares in the fable, who wished to know a little more about the noise behind them before they leapt into the pit in front. Theorists have even ventured to imagine that a clear perception of elementary principles tested by practical experience should precede action on a large scale. There have existed men bold enough to hint in private that work involving the most varied and skilful application of mind and machinery is no fit subject for amateur authority. It has even been asserted that in very complicated working conditions, if the skilled workman does not know how to do the work, at least no one else does. England has found her difficulty, and appears to be in a state of uneasy self-satisfaction about education.

2 Indigestion and crudities.

School-buildings are being put up everywhere. And if school-buildings are schools, be happy, the thing is done. There is much Inspecting going on everywhere. And if Inspectors are schools, be happy, the thing is done. Droves of children are driven in everywhere. And if droves of children are schools, be happy, the thing is done. There is much boasting of the money spent in schools, as if the more spent the better the deed, with somewhat the complacence of the millionaire, who glorifies his new potatoes because they cost a guinea apiece; but those who eat them are not quite clear whether the guinea-apiece glow, or the indigestion, is the right feeling. For indigestion there is; a great deal of it. The restless movements betray stomachs ill at ease. There is no peace. Everybody talks. Cabinet Ministers lay down the law. Philosophers lay down the law. The very school-boys lay down the law. And the public take sides with much vehemence. That is easy; for there are many sides to take. The congratulations of one Cabinet Minister are met by the sarcasms of another; philosopher finds philosopher bar the way; and partizans have every opportunity, that diversity of opinion and total absence of experience can give, of following their own predilections. There is however a general agreement in crying out for different novelties to be taught, without casting a thought on the question whether any real teaching is as yet possible; or even whether any power of teaching anything properly is in existence. There is a great cry for new subjects; but no voice raised for new teaching. Possibly because most people are acquainted with books; whilst the idea of

Schools are silent, gurgoyles spout. 3 dealing with minds may be unknown. At all events, known or unknown, no one names the unwelcome stranger. But there is much rushing to and fro, much confident action, much dead pressure, authority busy at work, and that general infallibility of dictation, which betokens a great outbreak with all its wants and all the inexperience of experimenting. It may seem curious that whilst this irruption has burst into the realm of school, overrun school-husbandry, and swarmed like locusts over the land, one voice has not been heard, and in one quarter a great silence has reigned. Schools have been invaded; schools have been operated on; and schools have been dumb. But it is not unnatural. The voice of the skilled workman, who has spent his life in trying to teach, finds nothing to invite speech. Their lips have been sealed. Why speak when so many are speaking? What chance of being heard, when everybody knows what no one has tried so much better than those who have, and who bring nothing but the harvest of their lives into the fray?

So no one, who has observed the laws of human action, will wonder at this absence of the skilled workman, for when the waters are muddied the fish are not seen. But mud is not reform, though often mistaken for it. A. sudden awakening to new needs in an old domain always creates this turmoil. Numbers have been pinched by the old, or felt the want of something new. The general carpenters of the universe are up and doing at once, eager for a job; all the clever ignorance of amateurs is in flood; aspirants for a name, and–a cause, see an opening; all the gurgoyles of the public buildings 4 The one-eyed man.

spout; in this way a movement is hurried on from outside with abrupt and prevailing power by those who feel all the inconveniences, and more, but know none of the difficulty. Like a large party suddenly discharged on an out-of-the-way Inn, everybody shouts, and wants, and expects everything, without the slightest idea where it is to come from. Those, whose business it is, have enough to do in doing what they can do for a time, without entering into discussions. So the schools have been silent, and busy; and perhaps not altogether unmindful of the true version of the old Proverb, "that in the kingdom of the blind the one-eyed man is hung." Nevertheless this present book, somewhat tempered by fear of the gallows, makes its appearance; and is a contribution, be it wise or foolish, from the side of the practical Teacher. Certainly it is an intrusion into the great company who have hitherto been eloquent on the question; and is not unconscious of a certain diffidence in the presence of so many distinguished personages. The Drawing-room assembly with its brilliant array of talkers is an imposing sight; and the fustian jacket of the working man looks somewhat out of place, and brings a sense of awkwardness to its wearer. Yet if work is the subject, and there is anything in knowing how to work, a working mans facts may be better than an orators words. They may serve to draw attention to things which have been overlooked; may put working necessities in a different light; and though they smell somewhat of oil and machinery may recall to more glib debaters that there is oil and machinery to be dealt with. The man who comes fresh from the work, and with some knowledge of what can,

A new despotism. 5 or cannot, be done with the machinery and material employed, and carries his work-shop in his brain, feels instinctively the gulf there is between himself and his well-dressed companions. He is utterly bewildered by the omniscient Babel around him. All his practical instincts are at fault. As he listens his solid experience seems to become a dissolving view, and melt imperceptibly away. He cannot build either theory or practice on the aerial foundation offered to him so confidently. To be silent appears cowardly. But how speak when the stored up gains of his life are put on a level with brain-spun gossamers, and carry less authority? It may be cowardly to be silent; but it casts a slur on life to condescend to speak on such terms.

The most important elementary truths have not been brought forward at all. No one has asked the simple question, what it costs to teach anything properly to each boy in a class. No one has examined whether it is possible under existing conditions to teach each boy. And of course the further questions, What is the percentage of untaught? what becomes of the untaught? and what becomes of the teachers, who have not time to teach, and never learn how to teach in consequence? have not come to the surface. The air is full of questions of principle, not one of which has been settled, though many are trying them unsettled, trying them in the most costly way. Vast systems have been set on foot. The land is full of new authorities; the land is full of new buildings, so different in kind that they cannot all be right. Large sums are being lavished, and for the first time in English History a despotic power is lay- 6 Our bigoted forefathers and Liberty.

ing down railroads for the minds of men, and insisting that all shall travel by their lines, and be taxed in the name of liberty and enlightenment to pay for them. Our poor old bigoted forefathers, who foolishly loved, and foolishly gave free gifts with a liberal hand to promote what they loved; and who calculated that in the long run freedom and love would produce the most loving and effective work, have indeed been convicted of folly. Liberty knows no such squeamishness; and they have been taught what liberty means. Their free gifts have been taken away; the one thing they loved most laid under a ban, and a policeman domiciled in their homes to teach them liberal ideas. This is a little puzzling to those who are not to the manner born. To some few it almost seems like a new bride in their dead mothers place; if indeed she is dead. But, dead or not dead, this new Liberty reigns, and every one who is not a fool does homage to the eldest child of advanced thought, which indeed has advanced so far that perhaps it has got quite round the circle again. The old Liberty is dead, the new Liberty reigns. And great are the acclamations, and varied the cries. Fustian-jacket does not know quite what to make of it all. There are so many surprises. A few of the rival cries shall be given to show that this perplexity is not an imaginary picture. To begin with, we are told boldly, as indeed we oughtto be told, that the people must be educated; and that no money can be better spent than the money which ensures that the people are educated. Everybody heartily, ex animo, body and soul, agrees with the great axiom. But here the unanimity ceases. What is education? Is it

Popes dictum. 7 the article now in the market? Who are the people to be educated? and how? These and many similar questions disturb the smooth perfection of the axiom quoted. "Knowledge is power" say some; get knowledge, give knowledge, and millennium begins. Others quote Pope with approval, or would do so if they had ever read him.

"A little learning is a dangerous thing,
Drink deep, or taste not the Pierian spring."

Which however may be common-sensed into plainer English thus,

"A little money is a dangerous snare,
Get thousands, but of sixpences beware."

Then a doubt arises whether the thousands are always better than the sixpences. It may be that a blind Samson pulling down the fabric of his home and his country on the head of all he loves best, amidst the congratulations of himself and his party, is less to be envied than the poor cripple, who, however misled, is too weak to do the same. All are agreed again that it is a debt owed to children to give them proper teaching. But who owes the debt? And, What is proper teaching? Do the parents owe the debt? and if so, at what period is it right and wise to make someone else pay it? In ancient times the enlightened Greek, or Roman, who was blessed with children, whom he could not feed, or did not want to feed, settled the question in a simple way, by exposing them. It was wrong, but logical, and effectual. Logical, inasmuch as no man has any right to call a life into the world which he cannot maintain. He is bound either to destroy it, or accept the cost of it. The sacred gift of 8 The endowment of beer.

life demands full acknowledgment. The ancients met the dilemma boldly by putting an end to the life. We demur to this. But was it the duty of the State to prevent this great crime by passing a law that everybody should be taxed to provide for his neighbours child, and remove the responsibility of life from the authors of life, by relieving the traitors against life from the penalties of treason? Or in plain vernacular, at what point is it right to make the moral, thrifty, patient worker pay for his idle neighbours illegitimate child, or illegitimate beer, or any other illegitimacies he may have a mind to? For that question lies at the root of all State support of those who dont pay by taxes levied on those who do. The mode of payment makes no difference. It comes to the same in the end whether a shilling is given under compulsion direct to the sturdy beggar who proceeds to spend it in beer, or the State takes it, as a compulsory tax, and hands it over to the alms-claimant, through some high-sounding title indirectly. The illegitimate child is supported by the thrifty mans earnings in both cases. No doubt the practice of exposing infants was cruel, nay criminal; but when ought the law to step in and punish the good man for his neighbours cruelty, and fine him for his own self-denial by making him pay for anothers self-indulgence?

The exposure of infants was got rid of in time but certainly not by laws compelling the community to rear them, as we are doing. No great natural law can be broken with impunity by man-made law, and some think, with St Paul, the duty of self-maintenance a great natural law, and that those who bring life into the world must

Education and natural laws. 9 bear the responsibility of their act. They want to know what is the difference in principle between the parents who expose the children they have brought into the world to the misery of ignorance and crime, and the parents, who in old heathen days brought children into the world with the same criminal neglect, and settled the matter by getting rid of them by exposing them to death. Are we to have State dinners, as well as State schools? State feeding shops for the body, as well as State feeding shops for the mind? A line must be drawn somewhere. Everybody cannot pay everybody elses debts. A line, they say, must be drawn somewhere, at what course in the State feeding is it to be drawn? at grammar? or at pudding? When does the law of robbing your thrifty neighbour, if he is in a minority, come in? And more important still, at what point does it stop? Is a man rich or poor who can afford to spend half his income on beer and maintain his wife and family with the other half, as contrasted with the man who spends 2 per cent, in drink, and has every penny besides preoccupied in struggling to keep an honourable position? Which of the two ought to pay for the others child? The experiment is not new. It has been tried on a grand scale. For a thousand years the civilised world strove to solve this problem. The Church in the name of religion and charity, whilst labouring with one hand, bribed idleness with the other, until the number of non-workers became intolerable, and the whole fabric broke up, and flooded Europe with unprovided poor. Yet at the beginning how beautiful the ideal seemed, how high was its claim. All the learning, and almost all the industry of their time io Thuggee sugar, took shelter in the monasteries, or roamed the world with the mendicant orders. But the canker of unearned gain proved too strong; a little spot at first, it spread till it tainted the whole; so all fell to pieces; and the problem of life, and how to deal with unthrift, began again. Various have been the remedies tried, the gallows, the guillotine, bribery, poor laws; and all have failed. Now once more, say they, the State steps in with the old nostrum new gilt, and proposes to endow idleness, unthrift, and self-indulgence in a disguised way; and establish new State mendicant orders in a mendicant school garb, of a neo-medieeval type. As if the taste of other peoples money ever left the lips that once have touched it j or ever failed, like the sacred sugar of the Thug, once tasted, to do in time its deadly work of robbery and wrong. Is the nation at a vast expense distributing Thuggee sugar? Many ask this question. Others again wish to know whether a little knowledge, even if honestly got, is the thing wanted; or if wanted, may not be bought too dear. The sixpennyworth of knowledge, derided by Pope, but not despised by common sense, may be too heavily weighted by its conditions. If bought by the sacrifice of independence it is too dear. A manly independence which faces its own responsibilities in a brave and honest way, is better than a little more learning with a pauperised heart, even if the learning is got. Character is worth more than sixpence, especially six-pennyworth of alms, a bit of another mans life in coin. No one can get from another what it is his duty to do himself. A man can no more do his neighbours duty for him than he can eat his neighbours dinner for him;

What has legislation to say?

a truth too often forgotten. And he who is master of himself and his passions does not want a beggars pittance from his neighbour to enable him to indulge his appetites at his neighbours expense. To put it in a different form; how many sixpennyworths of knowledge go to make a noble character? Exactly as many as the number of cannon that go to make an honest man. Power is not wisdom, nor knowledge honour. The distinction between help which is kind, and the pauperising, which is a cruel parody of kindness, requires to be marked; it is not yet done. The distinction between knowledge and training requires to be marked. It is not yet done. What is Education? We ought to know after so many years of legislation. Legislation is supposed to know what it is legislating about. The whole system of schools in this country has been reconstructed at a vast expense, much of it permanent and unchangeable. What answer have these architects of mind given to the great question which their reconstructive work supposes them to have mastered? Is Education the making the mind full? or is it making the mind strong? Is teaching the putting in facts, or drawing out and practising latent powers? Or is there something else not yet above the horizon?

Examinations and Inspection suggest a dark continent to the explorers foot. But one thing is certain. Examinations and Inspection proceed on the hypothesis that the work is known, and the process of working perfect. The Examiner, from the height of superior knowledge, only has to see whether the school follows out successfully a known and perfect method. A Government Examination and Inspection, with its overwhelm"

12 Examinations and perfection.

power both of the purse and of authority, runs all the work of all the schools before long into one mould; since anything original is outside the Inspectors range, any new method absent from his plan, any discovery wasted time in his court. Government Examination and Inspection, if they certify merit, imply a position of. perfection reached, and the clear superiority of the perfect judge over all he passes judgment on. But this implies death to all originality, and all progress of an original kind. Some say that the present processes are not perfect, and that there is no such superiority. Some think that liberty to improve is a valuable item in Education. Then again, what is Examination? on what principle is it to be conducted? Does any one know? We have not however yet reached the sagacious experience of Rome, so that two Examiners cannot meet without laughter. Our augury is still a science, and believed in. Is special teaching or general culture best? Bread-winning work, or mental gymnastics and brain-exercise? What necessities govern mankind in this field of labour? What natural laws are there which cannot be evaded or broken, however much men try? Natural laws, of the time that the individual can spare for self-preparation before he is forced to work for food; natural laws, of the strength of body and strength of mind that the individual brings to his task; natural laws, of the risk the individual runs of not succeeding in the higher kind of work, even if he can give time, and is fairly strong. All these, whether men like it or not, affect education, decide infallibly the main possibilities; and in the long run fix with an iron rigidity what different classes can do, and cannot do; and, unless

Education and trade laws. 13 a nation sinks to the level of the savage, by fixing this, fix the position of the classes as classes for ever. What is the unit of calculation by which in any given instance the cost of teaching can be calculated, on the basis that each boy is honestly taught, and neither the boy defrauded of his teaching because he is slow, nor the teacher of his pay? As far as teaching is a trade, the honest cost of the honest trade article ought to be known, and given. What then is the true price of a Teacher in the market? and why? If the true price is not given, somebody must suffer. And the further question arises, whether, if the teacher suffers, a system which requires martyrs to work it truly does not in the second generation get worked by cheats? If the taught, it is for the parents to consider whether the possible success of a few is compensation for the certain failure of the many. A thousand such gossamers are floating in the air, restless and intangible; up to the present time floating at random, merely cobwebbing the popular brain. Again, the power of the State to check all original progress, and kill by praise, is great. Can the State through any agency whatever award praise and blame year by year, and judge degrees of merit in schools without dishonesty? or can it only judge whether they are cut to the State pattern? How ought the Schoolmasters to be treated? Should they be made subject to their inferiors, and their skilled work placed under non-workmen? Through their agency thought and knowledge pass into every educated mind in the nation. They are the leaders of mind to the great majority. If the leaders are degraded will it benefit the led? And they are degraded if freedom is not given 14 A nation deformed.

there is no belief in skill; no trust that skill in the long run knows how to work best. It is easy to sneer at the word "leader," but it is a bad thing for those who sneer if the sneer is deserved; for the worse the trainers are, the more powerful is their effect. If the whole nation was passed through a system of Chinese foot bandages in childhood, what would become of our workmen and soldiers? But Schools do pass the whole nation through a course of bandaging; and if the bandaging is wrong the club-footed mind, with one perverted idea, like an excrescence, praised because it is unusual and artificial, becomes very possible. Supposing the due proportion between two great principles is lost, intellect versus character for example, and the intellect is fed at the expense of the body and feelings, the nation. becomes all head and no body, like a dwarf; and its leaders do incalculable mischief by having their humanity thus stunted and distorted, with much power, and little sympathy to make the power kindly. Or perchance the failures lose all sympathy, and gain little power, and become hollow-headed animals. The prize-winners big-headed dwarfs, the neglected boys hollow-headed animals, with no intellectual skill, and yet bred up to put faith in intellect, and to fall a prey in consequence to every talker of words, till a plague of words possesses the land. Once more, how ought the State to deal with the leaders of thought and knowledge? Should they be considered as skilled workmen engaged in work requiring consummate skill, who understand their work and are ready to do it? or, as carrying out the instructions of a higher authority, that understands the work, which they merely execute as instruments? If so,

The State and the Teachers. 15 who are these authorities that understand complicated work which they have never done? Are they Statesmen, or are they Philosophers? In neither case have they ever taught a child. Is it in teaching only that to have had no experience qualifies for being an authority? Or is the skilled workman interested in his work, or the unskilled workman not interested in his work, most likely to make the work prosper? If the Schoolmaster is not a skilled workman, who is? Who knows the work better, or is being trained to know the work better? Charles V. discovered at last that if a man could not make clocks keep time to a second, he was not likely to succeed with the far more varied machinery of mind. Query, Is this true or not? seeing that the school clocks will soon have to strike by St Stephens. Such questions require answering. They have not been answered. Nay, they have not, some of them, been asked. None have been considered judicially, on their own merits, apart from the pressure of the hour. These are a few of the loose thoughts that are running about, riderless. Many more might be found. But enough has been said to show that a great and undefined movement is going on in a haphazard and undefined way. Every earnest mind must rejoice that there is movement. There is life in movement. As long as there is liberty to move there is hope. If a strong new life is pushing out it needs space; space it must have, and space is cleared oftentimes by overthrow and pain. The war of opinions, and the crash of decayed glories, may be, and must be, full of trouble, often accompanied by great pain. There is nothing really to dread in this, if it is caused by the push of growing life. But true life grows from within 16 Good nets make poor gods.

outwards. When the stir takes place because force from without is breaking in, then there is danger. Then there is reason to fear lest no movement be tolerated out of the rigid line prescribed, and all liberty, all life, be put an end to. The watchwords of "Advance," and "Progress," are the true watchwords. But whether the result is true depends on the path trodden. Movement is not necessarily "progress," nor energy "advance." The Whither go ye, and how? are important factors. Without endorsing Popes absurd dictum about a little learning, many have serious misgivings whether we are not worshipping our nets, and doubt whether the new Gospel of the three Rs, which has so suddenly converted the most opposite parties, or even the Gospel of the whole alphabet, is quite so potent a miracle-worker as has been supposed. Good nets make poor gods; and the most valuable and necessary instruments are apt to disappoint their adorers when set up as ends desirable in themselves. There is room for doubt in the opinion of many whether the public have considered what they are asking for, or the value of what they are getting, when they cry out for knowledge. Rank and wealth, intellect, culture, and the public recognition of all these, do not prevent sometimes the owner of rank, wealth, culture, and reputation, from committing suicide. Will a feverish catching at the scraps of the beginnings of these make the poor man happy? Does the carting into the mind a few bushels of facts to be peddled out again make tne owner more of a man? Does any amount of accumulated brain-store, if that is all, make the man more of a man, or anything better than an animated knowledge-shop? There must be something unsound in the prescription of

Whether education has begun? 17 the school panacea to be swallowed like a bolus, whole, as the cure for all the ill that flesh is heir to. Men are wanted, what is it that makes a man more of a man? The three Rs, by themselves? God help men. Ignorance indeed has been tried now for many hundred years as a remedy for lawlessness, and has failed signally. Men are not orderly because they are ignorant. Obedience is the child of intelligence not of dulness. But though ignorance has failed to solve the problem of true life, a loud voice of clever violence, keen-witted crime, and voluble opinion, throughout all Europe is asserting, and is itself an unconscious example carrying conviction, that mere culture has failed equally, and large numbers are eager to upset anything and everything above them on this plea; whilst they consider throat-cutting the only cure for the cultivated classes. It may be that both sides are right, and both wrong; but at all events there are both sides. And power on the one hand, and numbers who claim enlightenment on the other, maintain each of them that the other is a failure. Such are some of the varieties of opinion and practice. As long as this is the case a confident foreclosing of the inquiry " What is education? " and, "How can it best be dealt with? " is not justified by facts. The question can still be asked, and can still admit of infinite discussion, "Whether education in any true sense has begun? " And it cannot be judged an unfitting subject for a working man to bring his facts and experience to bear on this. How can those who have never taught a child be authorities on teaching? Is teaching the only subject in which ignorance is knowledge?

CHAPTER II.

THE THEORY OF TEACHING.

27ie Philosophers Stone.

Knowledge is power, says the Proverb. Such is the general belief, and it accounts for the high value set on knowledge. For power is undoubtedly the ultimate test of the worth of all things. Whichever way it is taken this must be the case. The first originator of anything must be greater in power than that which is originated. Or again, the supremacy, which puts all things under its feet at last, must be supreme in power; whatever the secret of that power may be. The highest power with which we are acquainted on earth is life. No further proof of this assertion is needed than the obvious fact that man rules supreme over all the world in which he finds himself, by virtue of his superiority in life. His power of life makes him the master of material forces; his power of life makes him master over all lower forms of life; and superior power of life makes man himself

The great limitation: 19 master of men of a lower order. The aim of man therefore must be to attain the highest kind of life. And all the difficulties of all the worlds are solved as soon as it is known wherein true power consists. But first of all man himself must be considered, and the conditions of his existence which determine for him in what way, and how far, the pursuit of power is possible. Nevertheless as all men are men, and mans nature is common to all, there must be something in the life of all which under all circumstances, however varied, enables each life to be sufficiently trained in true power. Any true definition of power must apply to the life of every human being under all circumstances, or there would be forms of human life having no share in the common lot of human nature True power therefore must be that property of life which beginning with the lowest is exercised and trained in every individual, passing by an ascending scale into higher exercise as the life obeys and practises its laws more and more. To begin then at the lowest point. Before anything else can be done man must provide for his bodily life and its needs. This great limitation meets the ordinary ideas of perfection at once. These needs must be satisfied first. Till this is done nothing else can be done. The vast majority of mankind are compelled by the laws of nature to work for their daily bread, and always will be compelled to do so. This fact proves conclusively that the work for daily bread, since it is the natural law for man, and everything else is exceptional, is a noble order of life. What the race as a race is set to do must be a fitting exercise of the faculties of the race. The bodily life and its needs are so exacting that they 2O The saleable article.

demand most of the time that men have at their disposal, and will continue to do so for ever. The first form of power will be found here. Mans work, that is to say, the active and intelligent use of mans life, supplies these needs. The life itself by an exercise of the faculties belonging to life maintains the life. Accordingly in the first instance the ability to provide the sustenance of life, and all those requirements which are necessities in the complicated organization of civilized life, presents itself with a claim to be power. And it is a very true form of power. Its main characteristic is bodily strength and skill, employed either by a small exercise of mind, or by mind moving in very narrow limits. The body is the chief agent. This fact at once decides the class of power. Intellectually it is a low class, as comparatively little intellect is called into play in the first instance. Morally it is a high class, inasmuch as the body is the great touchstone of the feelings and emotions, testing and tempting, a perpetual referee in matters of right and wrong, the fierce exactor of work, and betrayer of the dissolute, the supreme arbiter, whether as servant or tyrant, of all mundane transactions, the teacher, which punishes with pitiless severity; the tempter, which allures with deadly fascination; in a word, the absolute determiner, according as it is dealt with, of the good and evil that befalls man, and of all the structure of the world made by man. Thus either in itself, or in the qualities called out by it, this work of the majority does give scope for all that makes life truly valuable, even though the market price of it may not be valuable. For this is its great peculiarity; it has a very definite market price.

Efficient life true education. 21

All these forms of work, and results of work, can be bought and sold. The market price therefore of any commodity, and the market price, that the man who produces any commodity can command, is the first test of value and of power; inasmuch as the price in the market is a rough and ready judgment on all the lower exercise of life, the work, that is, by which man is compelled in the first instance to get the means by which he lives, and to which he must turn his attention before he can do more; the work of the human race as a race.

Now power, or efficient life, is proposed as the aim of every true educator. And the market price of any product, or of the producer, is an important factor which cannot be left out in education. Whether the market price is high or low for the work done by any individual, no man can afford to keep all his life apart from it. No man can escape from its range. Few indeed are able to devote all their lives to mere research or knowledge. Fewer still would wish to stand aside, if they could, from all that their fellow men are doing and suffering. Market value meets the educator at every step as a most important factor in his search for power. There is no greater mistake than to disregard the natural laws by which life works; unless indeed it is exaggerating the importance of one or another part, and turning your hewer of wood and drawer of water into a god, because of the immediate advantage of his help.

Power therefore is the end proposed. But already on the threshold a great difficulty of determining what is power has appeared; and market price, which the majority would consciously or unconsciously elect, has been shown 22 The best life-power.

to have claims indeed but very imperfect claims. What then is power? Till something is settled on this question education is at a standstill, or blindfold. It is obviously the province of a teacher to know why he teaches, as well as what he teaches, and how to teach. Not unfrequently the first beginning of true work is a clear perception of the value of the work to be done, and the ability to excite interest by giving that perception to others. To leave for the present the dictum "Knowledge is power" on one side as an obvious fallacy, since to know without the power to use is possible, is common, and not unfrequently ridiculous; and passing by all other random dicta about power; the practical question presents itself in a very definite shape. The practical question is, What process will turn a man out best fitted to do life work, and enable mankind as a race to do their best? As definite a question as the question "What process is necessary to make a deal box?" And the first answer to this question is equally definite and clear; that process, namely, which best produces power in man himself, and makes him capable of employing his faculties in the best way. This gives a starting point at once. Power in a mans self is the work of education; and how to produce it the inquiry.

As this is a practical question, put forth with the intention of finding what a teacher and trainer ought to do in order to train the best men, by producing power in the man himself, and why he ought to do it? and how? a practical example of the commonest form of power, compulsive force, and its effects, will serve as a platform io begin on.

Parable of the Slave. 23

The slave toiling beneath his masters whip is a living parable coextensive with created things. It contains within its compass the whole problem of power; that is, of the right or wrong use of life. On the one side is skill and strength wielding the whip; and on the other an embodiment of life producing saleable work under the lash. And the vulgar call the visible Whip, and its influence, power; and the product, wealth; and the whip is an instrument through which the mind of the master works. In other words, there exists in the mind of the man, who uses the whip, a quality, by whatever name it may be called, or be it nameless, which comes to light in force, the force of the whip, or any other force that gives it expression. And the slave, a living being, has that belonging to him, which the whip and force can deal with; he obeys the whip; and the whip-holder is called his master, and is said to have power over him; and by this power gets a certain kind of marketable goods. So far all is straight-forward, and clear. He has power over him. But what power? and power over what? These questions require to be settled. There is the hard compulsive power of the whip, which man wields over man, on the one side; and there is the man who obeys the whip on the other. What then is the whip master of? It is master of a certain amount of movement of arm or leg. That is all. But a man is something more than arm, and leg, and body. What becomes of the man? At every stroke of the lash the real creature, as distinct from the working machine, hides itself. At every stroke of the lash, the love and hate, which is the man himself; and which, whenever he 24 The lash and life.

does mans true work, passes into that work, retires farther and farther into the depths of the cavernous heart out of sight. And the more the lash is applied the greater becomes the unapproachable distance between the master of the lash, and the real being before him, or any true revelation of the inner life of that being. The whip has power over an animated machine. But everything belonging to the being of a man as man; everything by which higher truths of the animate or inanimate creation are perceived and interpreted; everything in fact which makes man distinct from a moving animal, or even from a skilfully constructed engine, retires before the aggressive pretensions of force, and its stolid lash, into inaccessible fastnesses, unheeded, and despised; until in some hour of vengeance the pent up torrent of life leaps forth, and bears wild witness to the supreme energies of the inner being, which the kings of fools-paradise have long treated as non-existent, because they did not see it, and chose to consider their control over outward movement, power.

This is the great parable of force dealing with life, and the worth of life. All outward movement might be conceived of as carried out by beautifully subtle machinery. Few pause to consider what a vast amount of work once done by human hands, or living creatures, is now done by machines. In other words, machines have taken the place of man over a wide area, and in that area man may be looked on as non-existent. No one doubts that this process will go on, and that machines will take the place of man more and more in all external work. But it is easy in imagination to carry this idea further still, and with equal truth. There is a hard, Intellectual automatons. 25 mechanic power of intellect, which in theory always, and in practice often, is quite disconnected from mans real self, and his true nature as man. Professor Babbages calculating machine is an illustration of this. And following out this view, all work of brain that deals with any subject whatever separable from the qualities which make man man, and are distinctive of the excellence of humanity, can be conceived of as carried out by exquisitely subtle machinery. Marvellous automata can be imagined of force, bodily, and intellectual, able to carry on, when set in motion, every process of mechanical skill, every process of the visible structure of society and government. We are not without knowledge of this automatic action. What is instinct with its untaught, unteachable, inborn perfection belonging to all the race, always, but an example of a lower life endowed with faculties not only far exceeding those of mankind, but absolutely beyond the imagination of man to conceive how the action is caused? Consider the prophetic care of the white butterfly; how millions of butterflies, year after year, lay their eggs on the cabbage, with which they have no affinity in life, but which is to feed, when they are dead, the grub born from those eggs. Go to the solitary wasp, see him prophesy what is to come after his death, when he catches the green caterpillar, and performs that most delicate surgical operation with invariable success of stinging it exactly at the right spot with the right amount of poisonous effect to paralyse and not to kill; then see him take the little curled up creature, and pack him closely in the circular hole where his egg is laid, for use after his death. Observe the mathemati- 26 The automaton in Shakespear.

cal skill of the bee. Go build a nest, if you can; to say nothing of the power of passing by pathless ways of the carrier pigeon, the swallow, the dog, and innumerable other instances of the preternatural, with which we are so familiar that they no longer strike us as preternatural; and find yourself in the presence of a lower life gifted with a practical ability infinitely greater than anything that man with his higher life possesses; so infinitely greater, that human mind cannot discover, or frame any theory to account for it; whilst as far as the creature itself is concerned, to all appearance this ability is purely automaton work. Shakespear with his keen insight saw this fact of power apart from higher life, and has created such a feelingless living automaton. He has gifted it with marvellous powers. The elements and all elemental forces obey it; it rules as a king the material world; and though Shakespear has thrown round his creation the graceful fancy of a poets mind, and made it harmonise with the magic picture he drew, nevertheless Ariel is nothing more or less than an animated automaton, a creature without feeling, soulless, like the mermaid of Anderssen, or the German fictions, a beautiful embodiment of power, divorced from all that makes the life of man loveable, and tender, and true. Such automata however, as Shakespear has shown, would make a great show in the world. They would figure as external agents of a high order, busy with innumerable problems of calculation, statistics, science, marshalling other peoples thoughts, and exercising any kind of coercive power as well as all the fact-collecting power in the universe. But powerful, and honoured, as these auto-

The intellectual lash. 27 mata would be, they would be separated eternally from the feeblest, tenderest birth of human thought and feeling, requiring man to think it, and feel it. The distinction is very real; it is a most vital truth; and it cannot be disregarded in education. Mental factory wheels and the scintillations of life, are different in kind, and might belong to two different worlds, though both are packed together in mans being. So also with the power of the whip, which belongs to automatic brain-work. It makes no difference whether, as in the case of the master and the slave, the whip is in one hand and the work is extorted from another; or whether the whip-power and the work are in the same person. Whether the bodily needs and the great money-whip, or the lusts of the head and the great honour-whip lash out the work, the result is the same; though some whips can whip more out of a man, and get nearer to his human feelings than others. The hard will, however much the owner may exult in its action, is only a whip-power after all. This truth is the same truth whether force finds expression in the masters whip and the slaves work, when the work is exacted at the price of exile from all true feeling, all sympathy with the slave; or it is embodied in the forceful intellect tearing its way into the external knowledge of externals at the price of exile from life. The same law holds good throughout the whole world of mans being as an example of true life. The same law holds good in all creation where outward shape is, as it were, a body animated by the thought and life within, which have called it into existence, and have made it like a shell, holding, as a shell does, a living something within to which it 28-Life interprets life.

owes its existence. Let it be laid down once for all that wherever the hard intellect and automaton calculator has to deal with an array of facts, or with any external working of things, animate or inanimate, there the intellectual automaton reigns supreme. Again, wherever the hard intellect deals with the shell which contains the life, whether the life be the life of nature, or of literature, or of art, then also the intellectual automaton can do much, and seems to do still more. It can lash the outside, and get at all outside work, and be master of it, and enjoy the wealth and honour that the multitude always accord to the whip-holder, and visible strength. But man after all is the origin of everything done by man; and poetry, and prose, and painting, and architecture, music, and sculpture, as well as the food we eat, and the clothes we wear, are one and all embodiments of certain portions of mans life set in action. The moment a man puts forth anything in a shape, audible, or visible, he puts forth part of himself, a part of his mind, a birth of his life, and the ultimate judgment on all of it must be a judgment on mind, and life. And these mind-creations by their nature are subject to the same conditions as the life of which they are the outcome, and, as far as they go, represent it as faithfully as if they were separate living beings. If the automaton whip can whip its way into the slaves affections, then the intellectual automaton can whip his way into the other embodiments of affection and life. But all the delicate thought which is born into the world, all the glory of true feeling, all the subtle play of the higher realities, can only be reached by kindred spirit; and true life abhors

Mind-creations defy the whip. 29 the violence, repudiates automaton skill, loathes brutal strength of brain, and retires deeper and deeper before unfeeling force; whether the heart-truth be enshrined in the living body, or in that which the life has made, the painters picture, the speech of architecture, the melody of music, or words that burn, one and all are the language of an inward life; that is to say, are an inward life which has taken to itself a body. One and all are the offspring of travail throes, sweet or painful, of human parentage; and no one ever yet in all the worlds wrested a truth worth having from an unloving and unloved owner. The old, old story is as true now as in the infancy of time. The giants made war against heaven only to find themselves at last buried beneath a heavy load of earth. Giants, or pigmies, it matters not. And still it is the same:

"True beauty dwells in deep retreats,
Whose veil is unremoved,
Till heart with heart in concord beats,
And the lover is beloved."

Tender subtle feeling is tender subtle feeling, whether the words flow from lips beloved that speak them face to face, or whether they flow from lips, which in days of old gave them in trust to those dumb messengers, so faithful and so true, books, that from age to age keep safe, year after year, their treasure of enchanted life; waiting to be waked, whenever a true prince comes. The automaton intellect has no place here. The slave dealer might as well woo with his lash the love of the speaker of living speech, as the hard intellect expect to win its way 30 Wooing with the whip.

by force into the heart of the written thought. The fairy princess heeds them not. Both deal and deal successfully, if strong enough, with the husk and outside of that which they approach; both fail conspicuously, if not strong, even in that; and both stand for ever outside the walls of the home in which true beauty dwells and lives with those who love. A prayer for gentle, reverent, loving admission into the heart of that, which having been born of life, retains for ever the nature of that life from which it was born, must always be the beginning of true power. The humble watchful eye, which can recognise the existence of inner loveliness, is needed, if the learner is ever to read the high and varied emotions of noble minds, and by reading hope to kindle high and varied power in himself. This is a very practical question. The investigation has led to the recognition of three distinct forms of power, all of which however are combined in the perfect man, and are only misleading when separated. First, there is the mechanic power which does manual and bodily work that demands little exercise of intellect, or an exercise of intellect along a narrow track; this power is to a great degree amenable to force. Secondly, there is the automaton power, where the hard intellect assumes the mastery over the whole external world; but, as far as it acts alone, stands outside the whole realm of life and feeling. And thirdly, there is the living power of true. feeling, which is peculiar to man as man, and which uses the intellect as an instrument, and the body as an instrument, bringing into perfect harmony of glorious perfection the whole nature of man. Properly speaking the division is twofold, and the being of man comprises instrumental Instrumental power and living power. 31 powers of body and intellect; and living powers of love and sight, by which life sees truth with a mental eye, and loves truth. Love is not learnt. Love sees. Nothing can be more practical than this. Those who have followed the statement of facts already made, and who give their assent to what has been said, as a true statement of the facts of human nature, have already decided absolutely that all work which deals with the outer properties, and skin, as it were, of things, all carting in by mere memory of that which having been dropped in can be dropped out again, fails to fulfil the requirements of the higher training. And also, that all hard, unfeeling, irreverent temper unfits the learner, however strong in intellect he may be, for the higher ranges of power, which can only be attained by giving and taking the thrill of true feeling, and by an endeavour to enter into communion with the speakers however humble. These are truths, realities as certain as that the sun gives light. But both can be denied by the blind.

This most important definition of power as twofold, instrumental power, and living power, divisions of mans being, both contained always in greater or less degree, balanced or unbalanced, within man himself, establishes the first great proposition from which the higher education starts; and fixes on a firm basis both what kind of work it ought to do, and what its aim ought to be. Higher education must work on subjects that embody the higher life; and the work must be carried on with a view to beget and train the higher life. All memory work, as such, all the mechanic and skin-deep arts, by the very fact that they are only concerned with outside action, are 32 Love must woo work.

narrowed, each of them, to their own functions, confined within the limits of their own dexterity, represent nothing but an external need satisfied, and in no way carry their votaries into the true world of man, but stand outside the sacred circle of humanity, and only look in through a window at the place in which all that is tender, and true, and lovely, dwells, and will dwell secure, in spite of all efforts to break in. They do not therefore get beyond the outer court of Education, or compete as worthy subjects for the mind to exercise itself upon when the theory of teaching comes forward to be judged. Teaching in its higher sense is not concerned with any form of mere dexterity, however dexterous it may be. Yet it is well to remember that even the mechanic, and skin-deep arts and professions, being after all children of mind, do not drop all trace of their high origin; and, as far as they have sprung from true feeling and honest thought, demand the same kind of homage from those who would truly excel as the higher subjects do. The learner must submit himself to their sway. Even the shoemaker has his love for his work, the artist feeling, and the pride of skill, and would not sell the little fancy boot, " which he had made," he said, "in a moment of enthusiasm." Common work can be loved. All that is of life can be loved. And the village maiden must be wooed like a queen, if she is to be won; not in such courtly wise perhaps, but with as sincere a heart. And he, who would end with being true lord of anything, must begin by looking up with awe, and respect, and love, at the skill he hopes to win; and worship as above him that which he aspires to make his own.

The power of life. 33

Something has now been said of the region in which true power is to be found. Something also of the attitude of the true searcher for power. True power can only be found in the high er works of the higher life. The mechanic arts, and skin-deep specialities, and even the really wonderful feats to us, which can be conceived of as performed by an intellectual automaton of an Ariel-like capacity, or gifted with the unteachable perfection of instinct, have been set aside as too narrow in scope, and too much separated from the distinctive excellence of human life to come within the range of the best mental training, excepting as stepping stones to higher things. And the inquiry has been limited by this judgment to such works of life as man does distinctively as man, and not as an animal that moves. But what is life? And how does life act? The fact of life is so familiar, that a curious ignorance of what life is, is often found in dealing with life and its outcome. First what it is not. No subject which is put together piece by piece is living.

Life and living work has that within it which may sleep, lie dormant, but never dies, and which not only does not die but is a quickening spirit, acting like a germ in other lives which it reaches. There is a subtle play of life on life, a strange faculty of changing, and transmitting, and passing into whatever it really touches, to come out again in fresh combinations with a new birth of new creations and growths, all of which have a life of their own, whilst nevertheless all owe the beginning of that life to the germs they have received. In this way the whole world is incessantly interchanging for good or evil germinating ideas, which pass on, and on, and on, 34 Life in books.

sometimes traceable, sometimes not, but always in their aggregate growth forming the character of every nation, city, family, or individual. This is the essential power of life and life work, in which its transcendent claim to be considered the great practice ground of training and teaching lies. It is the most important factor of all in the sphere of practical work. And it makes no difference where the life comes from. Time, place, ages back in the old world, inhabitants of kingdoms long since gone, it matters not. The life influence is the same, and exercises the same procreative power in the same deathless way, whether it is clothed in the spoken word proceeding from living lips conveying messages of glowing life to ears that actually hear the voice; or whether it is a voice from–"the mighty minds of old"–a seed wafted down the centuries, with its seed-life in itself after its kind, floating, so to say, in the air, which lights, and takes root again; and when it takes root enters into the life it has touched, and becomes a new form of life, to go forth again on new missions. Life is ever acting in this way. The living thought and feelings of men live in the language of men; and literature is nothing less than the company, as far as the words reach, of those that spoke the words.

Words are the life. Because we have only a section of their lives in this way, which we cannot enlarge or change, the fact that it is living is often lost sight of. But the power it has of begetting life, its own life, in those who receive it, sufficiently proves that it is living.

Though like a seed, it must be planted, or it cannot change and grow, yet like a seed, when planted it does

Life undying, 35 change and grow, for the life is in it. Again the perception of life in books is much clouded by the fact that the glorious messages from the life of the ancient world have reached us in an obsolete shape; and the use of the term " dead languages" serves to darken the truth still more, and make the unthinking look on the literature itself as dead, and buried, and dug up out of the grave, a sort of mummy, curious, perhaps wonderful, but for all that dead, and past, and out of date.

Nevertheless it would be quite as absurd to talk of a dead picture, or a dead Cathedral, as of a dead language; if by dead we mean any diminution of vitality because of time. A picture is not dead because it was painted thousands of years ago. The paintings on the walls of Pompeii speak to us to-day with precisely the same meaning with which they spoke to those who saw them fresh and gleaming from the painters hands. The Nineveh sculptures give to our eyes their frank, bold message of hunting, or of war, with no less vivid reality than they did to the Assyrian, who put his mind into them first. The birds and animals on the walls of Egypt might have been painted yesterday, as far as their meaning goes. There is no death here. They are not dead, they do not die; the enchanted life remains for all who have power to break the spell.

Still less are the languages dead, with their great streams of life running clear and strong with unabated force, where he who lists may drink, and never find them fail. It pleased the old writers to take this imagery of a fountain ever flowing, and in no untrue parable draw from Helicon an inspiration of higher worlds, or 36 The creative energy of literature.

make Castalia flush their veins with divine pulsations. And flowers not of earth were gathered, fed by those sacred streams, and all their souls were bathed in the brightness of a better world, which they in turn strove to communicate to less favoured men. They saw this mystery of undying life, which yet is no mystery; they saw how it cannot stop, how it perpetually is born again with creative energy in some soul it has touched, and wherever it finds kindred life is absorbed into it, to come out again in strange marvels of new life working, as the old and the new blend, and shape themselves according to the latest possibilities of time into something never seen before, yet as surely life of the past, as it is life of the present, and has a present existence, and is going to breathe itself hereafter into the future also. This transmission of life from the living, through the living, to the living, is the highest definition of education. And the highest education and teaching must find its exercise ground in that region where the highest life is found. This is a self-evident proposition. Other works may be even more necessary, as bread is more necessary than Shakespear"s poems; but this necessity of first getting bread, and then getting house-room, and then getting this, and then getting that, however far the catalogue may be taken of things which have to be taught and done before the highest education begins, does not alter the fact, that the highest education must work in the region of the highest life. Now literature is the highest thought of the highest men in the most perfect shape. It is the life of the highest men transmitted. And this transmission of life takes place in any great degree through literature

Fructifying thought-germs. 37 only; that is, through words that have life, not metaphorically and in a figure, but as truly, whether spoken this moment, or a thousand years after the time when they first leapt forth from living lips freighted with a portion of the speakers mind. The power of begetting like feeling, and becoming incarnate again in living men never leaves them. Every generation by a familiar miracle receives the life-germs of the former world under new aspects of life, and with new generative energy. If it were possible to resolve to its elements the composite being of any educated man, what a marvellous revelation it would be of processes of implanted life. An infinite variety of living thoughts would be seen dropped in from. books, which then put out tendrils, and mingled in a thousand ways with the feelings and sights on every side, absorbing and assimilating nutriment from them until they became a growth of their own kind. Then, as time goes on, the growth is grafted and regrafted, and crossed and recrossed, with all manner of fructifying thought-dust, pollen from fields innumerable, and it all grows, and is pruned, as it grows, by experiences, that move living through the ages from the first utterance of primeval man, till at last it is gathered up into the powerful character of the educated man, able himself to become an originator of life to those who come after. Thus the old life is for ever entering into fresh combinations with the new, thought blending with thought, and spirit passing into spirit, until none can tell what part each separate influence has had in producing the final expression of power. All that is known is that life has been sowed, and grown into new forms of life. Such is litera- 38 Unconscious revelations.

ture at work. It would be a mistake however to allow ourselves to look upon the highest excellence attained as by any means the most interesting, or the most effectual of the workings of this life. A man can enjoy a landscape without being either a poet or a painter. There is much use in many things with little understanding of them. And without doubt this power of life penetrates down, and permeates social strata which are unconscious of its existence. A still greater number advance, with unwilling steps at present, but a little way. Yet this wide world, in which all the highest thoughts, the greatest deeds, the most noteworthy experiences of mankind live in a region of their own, is so remarkable a fact in the history of the human race, and in itself so wonderful, that to stand even on the outer edge of the magic circle, and merely know the existence of the kingdom within, lifts a man, even without any will of his own, into a different sphere. As standing on an Alp, and gazing into Italy, would of itself reveal another type of land to the most ignorant English villager, though it left him in his ignorance, save only the effect of that look. Perhaps the truth of this may be made somewhat more plain, by supposing for a moment, that by one sharp incision the knife of unpractical Folly could perform the operation of cutting out the whole knowledge of ancient existence, and Greek and Latin literature and art, with all their ramifications, from the life of the ordinary Englishman, and modern England. It is difficult to imagine what would be left. It is a patent fact that not one shoot of English higher life exists which is not traced back to roots of ancient life. Nay even if the minds of those

The philosopher s stone. 39 whom the actual knowledge cannot be said to reach were out of the atmosphere of that knowledge how stunted their lives would be. The whole nation would sink to a lower level, a level so much lower that it cannot be imagined. Our very language would be a different instrument, deadened, and blunted, with the keen edge of its meaning gone. The idlest, the most ill-taught schoolboy has that within him, which he knows not of, of this working of life on life. Even those who revile it know that it exists, and stand one inch higher by despising it even. That vast empire of glorious life in which all the greatness of the past lives and moves, is a realm consecrated to Power. Its boundaries are being extended day by day as life meets life and creates new life by meeting. It is hard, perhaps impossible, by any words, or any imagery to do more than suggest by far-off hints the eternal action and reaction of the thought-life, its ceaseless energy, its invisible magic, its all pervading presence, its complete mastery, its unity of continuous movement, in a word, its life. Mans knowledge of living creatures makes him limit his ideas of life to certain recurring types of body, unconscious that a creative energy has gone forth from himself, and is ever going forth,-which is not limited by the body, and exists independent of the lips from which in the first instance it was breathed, though always passing into human frames again. This life of living thought, which is both a disembodied, independent existence, and at the same time incarnate in bodily shape baffles mans expression, inasmuch as it is absolutely unique on this earthly globe. There is a subtle alchemy in life meeting life which finds no parallel 4O-The power-alchemist.

in any known fact. But the alchemists unconsciously shadowed it forth in their dream of the philosophers stone.

Life meets life in the living crucible of the mind. And all things thrown into that living fire are fused into a new creation. The philosophers stone is found, which has the power in very truth of turning all baser metals into gold. The philosophers stone is found in the great crucible of true education. The educator is a power-alchemist. He applies the flame of life, and man in himself becomes power.

CHAPTER III.

THE THEORY OF TEACHING.

Legs not Wings.

The object of education is to produce power in a mans self; and the distinction between mechanic work and life work, between automaton intellect and true feeling, forms the basis of educational science and of teaching. Like all great principles the more it is acted on the more practical its scope is seen to be. One consequence follows at once that life can only be trained to its highest perfection by processes of life. This decides that however useful, or necessary, certain forms of skill, and certain branches of knowledge are, they do not belong to the teaching and training of the higher life, because of the absence of the very elements of higher life in them. Bread is necessary, poetry is not neces-(, sary; but this does not make a baker higher than a poet., Nevertheless, in discussing education even well taught men constantly put the baker above the poet, and triumphantly close their argument when they have proved one 42 The baker and the poet.

subject more necessary than another, as if there was nothing more to be said on the question. It is however an absolute certainty from what has already been proved that the domain of life and thought must be the exercise ground in which any system of producing the highest intelligent power can be conceived as possible. And the highest thoughts of the highest minds put forth in the most perfect shape must be the study of all who are to be taught to think, and to put forth thought in shape. Add to this that all the knowledge of what man has done in the world also passes through literature, and is only received from literature, and the baker must indeed be above the poet if literature is not the main educational subject. But let us not hide the fact that the baker to the starving is above the poet. There must be people to do the low necessary work; and it is honourable work. Only it has no claim because it is necessary, and honourable, to usurp the place of higher things. That education will be best, which whilst ascending to the very highest begins at as low a point as possible. Here too language steps in, and claims the lowest as well as the highest place, so that it is no luxury of the few, but the daily bread of the many. The practical work to be done, and all the particulars and application of these elementary principles remain to be dealt with, and will be treated of in their proper place as each part naturally comes forward; let it however be laid down here, that the science of teaching, like all true science, comprises all subjects that can be taught; and is set forth in the best way, when it is first stated in the abstract, and then the noblest example is taken to illus-

Winning love by love. 43 trate its principles, and interpret its methods. Those who demand a small encyclopedia, and a varied range of technical instruction, are beside the mark. They must go to the retail shops and buy their special packets of knowledge. The theory and practice of teaching does not deal in such things. To resume. The main boundaries of education have to be made plain.

It has been proved that whip-power fails. There never yet was true mind-work born of life which mere hard force could reach. The limits are narrow indeed within which the whip is master; whether it be the whip of bread-winning, and the hard necessity of working to live, or the. whip of intellect, and the pride of strength. Force, and presumptuous superiority must be discarded for ever from the kingdom of life, and the learners world. Education requires that the right object shall be pursued, and pursued in the right way. The right object is higher life. What then is the right way of attaining higher life, since whip-power fails? The most complete definition of the right way is, the winning love by love. But this definition requires expansion, illustration, and practical handling. There are three gradations in love when a learner is in the case. First of all, docility; that condition of mind which presents no hindrance, but is ready in a confiding way to obey directions, and take the teachers point of view. Secondly, love of subject comes, when the learner has caught sight of the beauty of the life he is wooing, and gladly follows whithersoever he is led; and lastly, communion of feeling, when high and refined powers of heart and head combined meet on terms of equality the royal minds of old, wed them, and 44 Docility. Pre-working law.

become in turn parents of glorious births of mind; or at all events move amongst the highest forms of life with complete insight into their greatness.

Docility comes first. Perhaps the most practical form in which this can be stated is, that the removal of hindrances from the learners mind is the most important of all things for the ordinary learner and teacher. The laws which precede any work ought to be known, and observed. Very often neglect of pre-working law is at the bottom of the lifelong incapacity, which a little right instruction would have got rid of. As an example of the power of pre-working law a single illustration shall be given. The world of bare external fact shall prove how much depends on the position taken up before work begins; and show the momentous character of this fact in dealing with mind. Position is so important that it presents the paradox of many a problem impossible of solution to the intellect being solved at once by honest sight. Any child in this way may see and unravel the impossible. That which no calculation, no intellectual acumen can discover by brain-power simply needs no discovery at all, but is seen at once from the right point of view. But position, the right point of view, precedes work; and is part of that pre-working law, which no one looks to; and the unhappy worker is plunged into work without a thought given to him, whether his mind is ready to work or not. Let one example suffice.

Imagine a field of young wheat, and a man brought for the first time to see cultivated land. He would wish to know how such a crop was produced. Station him at the side, looking at it crosswise, athwart the ridges; and

The Wheat-field. 45 the hardest head, the most trained intellect ever owned by philosopher, shall fail to puzzle out any clue to the seeming confusion, the hopeless entanglement, the absolute disorder, that stretches before his eyes, for miles it may be, over the great green plain, and shall fail for ever. But a little child at the end of the furrows, following the plan of the sowers mind, from the sowers point of view, along the line the sower worked, simply sees at once, from mere sight, without any sense of puzzle, or any exercise of intellect, the whole order and design of the field. Such is the effect of docility, when mind submits to follow the track of mind, instead of setting up for itself, and working from its own point of view. The world has seen one very conspicuous instance amongst many of the value of position, and change of point of view in the realms of mind. The Ptolemaic system of astronomy was such a wheat-field. Men persisted in standing and looking crosswise at the starry universe, thick set with fiery seeds, with earth as their central point, because they had made up their minds beforehand that earth was most important; and earth was so great in their sight. But as soon as Copernicus discarded the self-centre, and took the childlike point of view, all the cycles, and epicycles, and endless entanglement disappeared. The universe no longer revolved round the earth; the earth difficulty was got rid of; and all became plain; as the earth was found to be a planet depending on infinitely greater powers than itself, and not supreme. Another form of wrong position is, when men make up their mind beforehand to search in a given region for that which is not there; as the astrologers did, who put life amongst the stars, and then 46 The disciple not above his master.

in defiance of common sense laid down laws of prophecy amidst the applause of mankind. Or as the biologists do, who put life in dying flesh, and hunt for it there, amidst the applause of mankind. These are some of the examples of the want of docility which takes the wrong point of view. But it is clear that the mind, which has produced any great work, knew what it was doing in producing it; and the right point of view for a learner must be the same as that of the originator. Or, in other words, the lower mind must follow the track of the higher mind, or fail in proportion to not doing so. This is a simple axiom; yet the observance of it would change the world. But if this is true in the wheat-field, and similar cases in the region of visible facts, which we call facts, as seeming to us most divested of ambiguous play of thought, the barest presentations of bare finality, how much rather will it be true in the great thought-creations, the intricate mysteries of feeling, the unique excellence of master minds at work, and in all things endowed with the changeful properties of life. The living being himself under the whip has already been discussed; and indeed no discussion is needed to show that knocking a man about does not reveal to us his inner nature, or win a way into his heart. In like manner the seeing a man daily for years is compatible with total ignorance of his real qualities; especially and certainly, when a lower and self-sufficient nature sees, and passes judgment on a higher. But many who dimly recognise this primary truth, that it is useless to kick a man if you want his love, which is only a forcible way of saying that the man must be approached from the right point of view, do not go on to the next truth, that the

The Cathedral. 47 same axiom holds good wherever thought and life has been at work. The question always is how to get at the inner reality. In the case of the wheat-field merely standing at the right end was enough to reveal the sowers mind and the whole plan of the sowing. Let us proceed a step farther in the same direction and examine when a subject is manifold and complex, requiring love as well as knowledge to master it, in what manner love as well as knowledge can be produced. For although there is no philtre that can inspire love as fables have said, nevertheless there are certain conditions which must be observed before love is possible, without which love cannot exist.

A great Cathedral is an example of the most visible and material kind of a complex subject. It is a glorious specimen of thought in stone. But to many it is only stone. The stone meets their eyes, and brings no message of the higher life, though it is a most true and living expression of higher life. There it stands for all to see, vast, immovable, majestic. What is the point of view from which to examine it? It strikes the eye as a great building. As a great building it shall claim attention first. The outward form, as it strikes the eye, shall make the first appeal. To begin with, it must be seen. An innocent looking statement, but really containing within itself the whole question involved. When a traveller in the distance, coming to see it, crosses the last hill, ten miles off, as he moves slowly over the ridge, the massive walls and towers come into sight; and the great fabric in the middle of the plain tells him that he has before him the famous work of the days of old; and there are just sufficient characteristics, (sufficient expres- 48 Seeing from a distance.

sion of thought that is) to mark it even at that distance as a building intended for worship. Well 1 he has seen it. He turns round, and goes home, and perhaps recounts to the world his infallible judgment on what he has seen. For it is those who see afar off that are infallible. Such conduct put in this concrete form seems absurd. Yet so far from being absurd, all the infallible wisdom, and most of the knowledge of the world is of this kind. Men see a great something afar off, and are satisfied at that point. Mere distance deprives them of any power to see more; and many do not want to see more, and never go near enough to get fuller knowledge, though what they do know may be as familiar to them as the palms of their own hands. Many have not time to see more; many have not strength to get nearer; and so it comes to pass that three-quarters of the knowers always keep their minds ten miles off their subjects, and discourse glibly from that distance as if they knew all about it, really deceived sometimes in this, because what they do know they know so well. But the feeling of a person ten miles away for the Cathedral is clearly of a very different kind, however intense the seer may think it, from the feeling of one who goes closer. Let us advance five miles. At a distance of five miles an entirely new idea is put before the mind by the mere change of place. The Cathedral has now become an important feature in the landscape; and a painter could paint a beautiful picture, in which the Cathedral should greatly add to the beauty, and recall many tender recollections to those who know it; but all the time the landscape, not the Cathedral, is the main consideration still. The fact how-

A new world brought close. 49 ever is clear that the space of five miles has put an entirely new creation of Cathedral before the mind. Many minds always stop five miles short of their subject, and are satisfied. In this case, as in the other, what is known is known most definitely, the amount of knowledge makes the difference, not its distinctness. The first seer is justified in being quite as positive as the second over what he does know, if he is content to keep to what he does know (a useless hypothesis; none ever do). But this positive imperfect knowledge contains just so much truth as to deceive many. If the last five miles are passed the same entire change of mental power takes place again. In the precincts all the outside is clearly seen, and there is nothing else, the landscape has vanished. The mind is filled with the great stone personality, which stands out large and strong before the eye to the exclusion of every other object, and the whole Architecture, its beauty, its variety, its marvellous construction, its manifold triumphs of art, at once take possession of the spectator with a completely new set of facts, and another world of ideas; and he becomes by merely standing there endowed with new perceptions of the great creation of life and thought, which the Cathedral existence embodies. Such is the power of getting nearer and nearer to any work of mind. And it makes no difference in the fact of increased knowledge that sight and nearness is sufficient to give it. In other words the effect is the same whether supernatural power of sight, and wings lift their possessor into a new world, or the new world comes down close to an ordinary mortal, and reveals itself by being brought close. If a man 50 The true disciple gets inside.

can with ease get into a new world by walking ten miles, he need not sit still and maunder over not having wings. Our new Cathedral world has been reached by feet, but we are still at the outside. Many are satisfied with a definite knowledge of the outside of beauty. But the inside has yet to be seen. And the great purpose does not reveal itself till the reader of mind addresses himself to the inner truth; and lovingly with a disciples heart and eye, searches out the history, learns the plan, strives to enter into the secret shrine of the feelings which wrought out the great sanctuary, and to translate out of the stone the speech which in very truth is in it. Once more mere change of position has brought entirely new perceptions of an entirely new creation to the mind. The true disciple, with the loving heart, who has the feeling which takes him into the shrine within, deals with a different set of facts, and is enriched with infinitely increased power of sight by merely getting closer to the great work of mind. Then as he gazes, spirit answers spirit, the glorious poem languaged in the stone breaks forth into a silent chant of life, voiceless thoughts breathed out of the fair structure pass into the gazers soul and enter there, and there revive the memory of noble minds, that built their hearts, their blood, their all, into those walls. He holds high converse with the dead that live. All the inventive genius wakes at the thrill of a loving touch. Prayers that passed upwards from praying hearts, and as they passed upon their heavenward message were petrified in pinnacle and lofty roof, pour forth their inspiration and their faith once more. Anthems caught in mid air, rising triumphant towards the throne of God,

Mind reads mind. 51 column, and arch, one blended harmony of praise and worship, peal their great organ pipes for him whose life interprets life; and roll down all their music, from the eternal stone, the secret marvels of the old, old years, the charmed speech of ages dreaming there, there dreaming in each sculptured coign and niche, so silent yet so ready with their story. Een thus the dumb walls speak, and the beam unlocks its secret, and the shut cabinet of spirit-knowledge ever opens to a spirit-power, that can watch, and wait, and learn. Solitude is there no more. Unseen presences sweep to and fro, the void space fills, the solid buttresses and towers melt back into the aspirations out of which they grew. The living growth proclaims its life. The great past lives again, the peopled centuries unfold, and throng the quiet scene with countless shapes, as mind reads mind, content to honour, and love, and follow, according as it is led.

Such is the power of getting near, the power of the right point of view, when distance is got rid of. Let it be assumed that the mind of the spectator receives no further training, and is not endowed with higher powers by right action, still the great fact stands out with unparalleled significance, that every advance brought an entirely new and higher set of ideas into sight, and that the mere seeing the new creation of nearer sight put the seer in possession of a new world. Let us carry this a step further into the domain of the actual life of man. Take a homely illustration of this. There is a little country town with its unlovely street of flattened houses of dreary brick, passed through day by day by one whose life work takes him farther on. The same dull picture 52 Bricks or realms of love.

year by year stamps its familiar knowledge on his mind. Bricks and windows, windows and bricks, with occasional glimpses of faces at the windows. And so it might go on for ever, if life lasted for ever. But a day comes when one of the unlovely houses in the unlovely street, which he has despised the sight of, opens its doors to him. He has received an introduction, and he goes in. There is a family, an island of life within the bricks. A beauty and excellence of noble life is there. The dull brick house is brick and dulness no more. Again and again those scornful feet forget their scorn, and are drawn irresistibly into the charmed circle; till by degrees for him all loveliness and truth seems centred there. He learns to know it more and more; the whole world becomes glorified by love and life; the spot is sacred evermore; it holds all he cares for this side the grave. Such is the transforming power of life, and love, and admission into realms of love. Once more the power of getting near, mere change of position, changes the world, and opens new possibilities of learning, whilst the power of loving with which the getting near endows the humble loving mind enables love to win its full return. And this law holds good throughout creation.

It holds good with living beings. It holds good with all things put into shape by living beings in speech, or sound, or action. All languages, spoken or unspoken, languages that speak to ear or eye, are interpreted by this law of procedure. This law holds good with the great unspoken language of the voice of God in Creation.

Mind must touch mind.

The burglar weds not queens. 53 It follows from this that the burglar, who thinks to break in by force of intellect, and wrest the secret power of such a spirit-home of beauty from the spirit within, is little likely to win the queen who dwells there in her home. The burglar intellect will be an outcast ever from the home of higher life.

There is no mystery in the matter. It all follows a well-known track. Love must woo love, the loving mind of one willing to be led gets closer and closer to the object of its love, ever clasps with reverent affection the beauty it would fain make its own, and strives to interpret every great work, be it in stone, or a painting, music, poetry, or prose, or any form which noble thought of God, or man, has taken, by this same law of interpretation, the only law that thought-creations obey. This is simply the teachers starting point. He has got a clue, a method. The way is cleared of vain excuses for idleness, and vain boastings of cleverness. The practical results of this definition are of the highest importance. Not least of these results is the fact disclosed, that the work to be done is possible, and can be done. There is hope for all.

Half the bad work of the world arises from want of hope, not from want of vigour. That Will-o-the-Wisp hight "cleverness" in schools, and "genius" in more sapient regions, has tricked more into "the filthy-mantled" pools of conceited ignorance, or hopeless despair, and stopped more work, than any other cause, besides being at the bottom of much false teaching, and luring nations to their destruction by false glitter. Prizes, which few can win, are dangled in the air by public opinion.

54 Genius stoops to conquer.

Thence comes a fatal facility for skimming over the surface, and playing with flowers, and a reputation for cleverness, which satisfies many into a life-long lunacy of pretentious folly. Still greater numbers sit down with folded hands, and will not try to move at all because they lack the Will-o-the-Wisp flash, and whether they idle, or despair, agree in the sitting still, and the folded hands, and the excuse "it is no use, they are not clever." And the teachers leave them untaught, as by theory of Will-o-the-Wisp is reasonable; and the parents acquiesce in this, and support the practice, a fact which by any theory is unreasonable.

When we consider the deleterious fumes that have been let loose about genius, and the windbags that conceit is for ever untying amongst the children of men, it is a disenchantment, but a pleasurable one, to find that whatever genius may be, it is not anything supernatural; it is not being born with wings whilst ordinary people have only legs; but it begins at all events not by soaring above other men, but by coming down, and kneeling, and supplicating, and winning a way in, and nestling at last in the inmost heart of spirit-power, and learning all its tenderest perfection by devotion to its service, patient, watchful, long-suffering devotion, and without this there is no genius. But if genius thus stoops to conquer, and cannot conquer without stooping, then any mind can stoop in like manner. Whether it has the final conquering power in it, or not, it has at least the power of beginning on the same track, and following the same track, as far as its strength will carry it. If genius, true genius, is thus shown to begin as a most sober, working-

All have legs. 55 day possession, then everything below genius comes more and more within working range, and the learners bugbear, or excuse, want of cleverness, disappears. The wing theory is convenient for idle learners, and incompetent teachers. For what is the use of trying to fly if you have no wings? or what is the disgrace of not flying? So it comes to pass, that all unpalatable work soon falls under the head of trying to fly, and one sweeping absolution of " no wings " gets rid of the undone task, and the shame of not having done it, both for the master and the pupil. But a true insight into the nature of genius, as the faculty that begins by loving exceedingly, and getting close through love to the noblest forms of life, makes the power of coming close, not the power of soaring, the prevailing power. Here is solid ground, and right good foothold. All can walk part of the way with genius.

There is no such lusus naturx as a winged breed of mankind disporting itself above the wingless crowd. There is a path, which all must tread; and all have legs. Some move quicker than others, some more slowly; but all can move.

CHAPTER IV.

THE THEORY OF TEACHING.

Stupidity banished.

We have arrived now at the definition of the right point of view for teacher and taught. They must endeavour to win true power by humbly striving to get close, to win a way by love into the heart of the subject they deal with. The theory of wings, and soaring, and the ethereal, and the empyreal, may now take refuge in the hallowed precincts of Cloud-Cuckoo-land, so considerately provided for it by the poet of old. It is a comfort to find there is no need of flying; especially for those who are unconscious even of the gentlest titillation of nascent wings. Having got rid of the cuckoos with their iteration of their own name, let us proceed to examine what genius really is, or in other words what is the highest form of working possible for man; and how far it is amenable to teaching.

The right point of view for all work has been discovered. It is the getting under, not over, the subject,

Eyes shut, ears closed. 5 7 and working upward, and inward, closer and closer, by loving observation, to that which has to be known. All power begins by loving observation. This will appear more and more clearly the moment practical work begins. Every work, especially works of genius, must be the result of thought. Where does the thought come from? Evolving camels out of the inner consciousness has been justly ridiculed in the well-known story. But nevertheless there is no fallacy that inhabits more doggedly the youthful cranium than this, none which the teacher has to meet so often, either not noticing it if his time does not permit, and his knowledge, or incessantly wearied by its reappearance in spite of precept, perpetually at it, like a thrush with a refractory worm, half of which it hangs on to, whilst the other half slips back into the hole again. Beginners always will insist, when told to write a descriptive narrative, in getting into a corner, shutting their eyes, as it were, and forthwith evolving out of their inner consciousness. Beginners always will insist, when told to construe, in imagining what the great writer ought to have said (poor old gentleman!), and forthwith proceeding to give out their version, in total disregard very often of the words beneath their eyes. And what shall we say? The schools of the Prophets have not perished. Bear witness those innumerable soothsayers, who, trusting solely to the power of divination, boldly set forth the unknown day by day in guesses, that are at once marvels of folly, and alas! of a habit of mind that defies teaching. The refusal to observe, the dogged obstinacy with which they cling to the "wing" theory unconsciously, is the most remarkable fact in a teachers experience of mind 58 Something to think about.

Yet even then, where does the material come from, flimsy as it is, which they produce? If we imagine a man deaf, and dumb, and blind, endowed with the highest natural powers of mind, such a being with all the avenues of observation closed would remain a hopeless blank, practically an idiot. His ear would bring him no messages on which to employ thought; no sweet voices of his kind would stir his pulses with joy; no music of bird, or any sound, would break the ghastly silence of his soul; his eye would gather no harvest of delight, or terror, his lips could not utter any impulse from within so as to become a moving power. Thought, as we speak of thought, would be impossible, for–it would be impossible for him to collect any material to think about. "Material to think about." That is the heart of the whole matter. There can be no thought without material for thought. The baby with its wondering eyes for a time gathers material even as it takes food, by a natural process. It cannot help doing so. After a time the curiosity excited by novelty without, and by life within, is somewhat satisfied by familiarity with the outside of the objects most often seen, or repressed by contact with ignorance, and commands to stop unwelcome questions. At this point, where the first curiosity ceases, true education begins, by lifting up a little corner of the veil of the world of common things, and showing that there is an inside as well as an outside to be seen. Thus observation instead of curiosity, or rather as a trained development of curiosity, begins the work of intelligent progress.

The first advance on unconscious absorption of material of thought is the implanting a habit of observation,

Turner and stone-throwing. 59 that is, of consciously gathering material for thought. Here again is solid ground and good foothold,–leg-work, not wing-work. Observation is only a better name for patient well-directed work, a name for learning to see by getting close, and waiting long on that which is worthy of being known.

It is recorded of Turner, the great painter, that he was seen to spend a whole day in throwing pebbles into the water, whilst others were working away round him. Throwing pebbles into the water! With what contempt a machine-intellect with its mechanic power of turning all things into a kind of philosophic ledger, would visit such a childish proceeding. How the cold, calculating fact-machine would scoff. But there are worlds on worlds; higher worlds with their inhabitants; and lower worlds with their inhabitants; and the great painter working in the world of life, and living thought, knew what he was about. His power of observation was so great, and his patience and love so unwearied, that with his trained eye he could find intense interest, and gather lessons above all price from the ripple, and the waves, and the play of light, and harmonious discord of varying movements from the common curves, made by a common stone, falling into common water; over which an untrained eye and mind could not spend a profitable moment. Before his eyes was spread the ever stationary, ever moving mirror, the changeful eternity of light that flows, the gliding earthborn light of water, with its strange memories of higher worlds, and strange affinities to cloud and sky, free beyond all earthly things to come and go, still loving to borrow, as it moves, brightness from sky, 60 The prophet voice.

and gleams from cloud, or shore, and welcoming in its bosom, like a living thing, all images that reach it in its course; he stood and looked upon it, and tried to unlock its secrets, and conscious, or unconscious, of the full interpretation, caught some glimpses of the great illuminated text of the book of the thoughts of God, appreciated the exquisite subtlety of the handwriting of speech divine, became a kind of living microscope in the power of seeing unknown beauty, and then handed on to us non-seers the gain of new discovery to be henceforth part of the possession of the world. A common stone thrown into common water could thus become a prophet revealing truth. But to whom does the prophet voice of stones and water speak? A careful analysis will shew that the great painter, the genius, could see and understand, because he had learnt by years of patient work to observe more than other people. The child begins its first attempts at drawing by a few bounded lines from an unpractised hand, that will not do its owners bidding, and an unpractised mind, that as yet has not much bidding to give; and under it he writes, cat, or dog, or cow, as the case may be, and the writing is necessary. And unless hand and mind practise, that is, work, they will never do more. Turner himself, had he been debarred from practising his hand, and not permitted to exercise his eye, could have done no more. It is quite immaterial to this argument what the difference may be between any pupil and Turner before they end; the all important fact remains, that for a long time the path of both is the same; and the still more important fact, that the teacher has as his province

One path for ail. 61 that path, and that path only, as far as the external aspect both of his own, and his pupils work, is concerned. The teacher has no concern with the beyond; but the fact that the vast majority never get within sight of the point where a beyond begins, but remain in the limbo of little-boy drawings, and such like, does concern him very much indeed. The point at which observation begins, and at which it stops, a point very often but little in advance of the unconscious vision of the child, is his business. The teacher is disgraced when all the result of his so-called teaching is the commonplace production of the commonplace features of their profession by men who are supposed to have been trained. This is not the way that genius acts in achieving greatness. The great man quickly masters the commonplace outside and husk of things, and goes on, and perseveres, and penetrates into his subject, and loves it, and sees more than others because he loves it, and strives to reproduce what he sees. If a painter, he copies, and copies, and copies art and nature, with ever increasing skill and insight, till his inner consciousness is filled with images capable of being made use of at any moment. If a poet, he turns his eye, and all the strength of his passionate, impressive heart, on those objects which stir his inmost being, because his inmost being answers to their life; and they throb and thrill in union with his feeling, filling his soul with music half his, half theirs, a new. creation of melodious thought. And so on through the whole range, down to the schoolboy in the lowest form, as far as any true work is going on. Aye, true work; loving work that is, not the clothes and the body, the garments of the man himself alone 62 Genius defined.

present, but all his love, and all his strength; true work, that is what it all comes to; and Carlyles definition of genius with a slight, but all-important addition is complete.

Genius is an infinite capacity for work growing out of an infinite power of love. Take courage each and all who have any feeling. Powers spring from love. When you find that you have something dear to you, which is dull and dry to others, but which you clasp close to yourself with joy and yearning; when you have a love of some seeming insignificant thing of creation and mind, and feel that life may be worth devoting to it, know there is within you the beginning of power. An acorn is planted in your breast. When your heart as a child has any vivid feeling of joy, or sorrow, longing or disappointment, do not crush it; master it, but do not crush it; master it, study it, endeavour to quicken it into more life, always mastering the emotions produced by keen and impressible perceptions; cherish the impressible and keen capacity of feeling; it is an acorn planted in you; it is the beginning of power. All the great men that have lived have acquired greatness in the same way. They observed, they worked, they loved. Observation is work, and true work lives by love. Without observation there is no thought; without the material for thought there is no building. Whether it is pleasurable, or otherwise, poets, or school-boys, observation is work, and true work is love moving, and the ideal, after all that foggy enthusiasm can do to mystify, or blowers of glittering bubbles can blow, is but the final expression of the highest thought produced by the greatest knowledge and

Observation, work, love. 63 feeling; and the greatest knowledge and feeling is produced by years of patient loving work in a mind originally strong and susceptible. No doubt this is a most unsatisfactory conclusion, and prosaic, for angels, and wings, and the empyreal to arrive at, most unsatisfactory for the idler, the fool, and the vainglorious; but intensely comforting, and happy, and real, to an earnest man, who is ready to humble himself to watch and wait on what he loves. Above all, it is intensely practical for teacher and taught. The path is clear; the possibility of moving is clear; the goal is clear also. It gives the certainty of success to all without exception, who are willing to tread the path. Observation, work, love, these are the masters of the world. The teacher, who is a true teacher, knows what he is about; and, if he is allowed to work, and external laws do not stop him, can do it. So can the taught. Observation, work, love. By these that high training is built up, which deals with life and mind as all other pursuits are dealt with; and learns faithfully from the first rudiments to the complete end; and no more thinks it beneath his notice to do the lowest kind of work, than a musician thinks it beneath his notice to know his notes.

But if this is the process by which mind reads mind, anyone can begin to do it. The loving eye and working hand of genius can be acquired in some degree by all. There is no more stupidity in the common acceptation of the term, no more incapacity to do well, no contempt on the one side, and despair on the other: all can be taught to observe, some more quickly, some more slowly, but all can do it. Learning is but walking, 64 No cripples, no wings.

putting one foot before another, and all have serviceable legs.

There are no cripples; far rather the great majority are active-minded enough by nature. On the other hand there are no wings. The excuse of the idle pupil, and the incompetent teacher, does not exist. Work; simple, straight-forward, intelligent work is everything. The strong and the weak alike, the genius, as well as the slowest mind, must go through the same work, till they part company, as perseverance, strength, and love carry the best minds farther. There can be no thought till there has been observation. There can be no observation without work. The highest form of human existence is the power of working unweariedly and prevailingly lovingly wooing, and winning, power by love. One word, rightly understood, contains it all– Work.

CHAPTER V.

THE THEORY OF TEACHING.

Market Price, and Real Value. The Auctioneers Hammer, and the Swine-herds Horn.

It is useless pumping on a kettle with the lid on. Pump, pump, pump. The pump-handle goes vigorously, the water pours, a virtuous glow of righteous satisfaction and sweat beams on the countenance of the pumper; but–the kettle remains empty: and will remain empty till the end of time, barring a drop or two, which finds its way in unwillingly through the spout.

This is no unfair picture of what is going on in the school-world to a great extent. The whole theory and practice amounts to nothing more than a pouring out of knowledge on to the heads underneath. Let the question whether this is the right method of proceeding stand aside for the present; and the effect on those who are subjected to the process be considered. The people pumped on do not like it, and, as soon as they can express an opinion, show they do not like it. And they 66 The kettles and the deluge.

shortly pass into the ranks of the uneducated, who, because they have been pumped on, think they have a right to express an opinion on education. That opinion is not favourable. Many have got next to nothing, and, both by example and precept, inculcate the uselessness of what they have gone through; or its luck; that it is a lottery with a few prizes, and many blanks. Their sons go to school again, inoculated already with these ideas; and thus, generation after generation more and more closes its mind, and learns to disbelieve in any certain gain. Generations of pumpers, and pumped on, turn out generations of drenched, confused emptiness. And this empty, much-enduring race offers a passive resistance that is quite effectual, and is impervious to all ordinary efforts. But pumping, and being pumped on, is not teaching and being taught. The shut mind defies all such attempts to reach it, however zealous, or skilful in their way they may be. Nothing can be done as long as the lid remains on. But why do the kettles keep the lid on? and how can the lid be got off? The kettles keep the lid on because they do not believe in the deluge. Before any teaching can begin, the teacher must know what has to be taught; and the pupil must know that he can get it, and that it is worth having when got. Here is the evil of the pump. Not the emptiness, but the disgust and unbelief in training is the fatal legacy the pumpers leave to those who come after. No skill, even when there is skill, can reach a boy, who hates what he is set to do, who does not believe in the value of it, who does not believe that he can get it even if it is valuable. The ignorance of the untaught would be of little consequence

Abolish the pump, train. 67 if they believed in teaching. But pumping is not teaching. Dropping knowledge in is not calling latent power out, when knowledge is dropped in. Being pumped on induces despair or hatred, or both, in the great majority, and a low view of education in all No teaching in the true sense is attempted, no idea of teaching is received; what wonder if the pump succeeds in convincing the young that trying to get knowledge is a hopeless and disgusting task; and the value small. A profound ignorance of work, and its value, possesses the schoolboy-world quietly entrenched behind all the natural repugnance to exertion, and guarded by all the temptations to play, or worse, which swarm round boyhood thick as flies in summer. It has already been shown that nothing is required in a true system of education which the beginner cannot do. This is the first step. The work is possible. The work is valuable is the second. The learner must be got at. This is the way to get at him. Abolish the pump. Deal with each mind. Destroy the idea that knowledge is all in all. Train. Make the learner know the value of training. Make him see that what he has to do is worth the pains bestowed on learning to do it. The life of a nation turns on convincing everyone, first, that education can be got, and secondly, that it is worth having when got. It is not too much to assert, that the great majority think truly that education at present is a lottery, and that many think it not worth having. The question of value is indeed important. Every boy ought to know the value of the work he is set to do. Scraps of knowledge, the cold victuals off other mens trenchers are not valuable, and they are not nice.

68 The chimney-sweep envied.

Many years ago, one spring morning, in the pleasant southern shire, when the sun shone out on the happy fields, and touched with loving care the gables of my home, well do I remember how I saw, through a film of tears, a little chimney-sweep come up the road leading to the house, and envied him with passionate envy; for he might stay, he had not to go to school, as I had, he was not banished. In Romeos words, had I but known them,

"Every cat, and dog,
And little mouse, every unworthy thing;
Lived there in heaven, and might look on it."

But I had to go. It is easy to laugh at a childs sorrows, but they are very real. That morning more than fifty years ago, though many a bitter day, and fierce hard year has been faced since, still lives in memory as full of pain; that hour still holds its own as not the least wretched of unhappy times. And indeed in the little bounded world of the childs life there was only too much cause for the feeling, very real grounds for that emptiness of heart. School meant nothing less than light-hearted liberty gone, and a prison in exchange; where every joy, which at that time was joy, was shut out; a prison full of blind fears, daily task-work, sharp and constant checks, accompanied by absolute ignorance of the why? and the wherefore? From beginning to end the whole thing was a painful puzzle, a riddle without an answer. The envy of the chimney-sweep has not passed away out of the boy world, though most boys pitch their ambition somewhat higher in these days. Most assuredly the aimless riddle is as obtrusive, and

Value, elementary questions. 69 unanswerable as ever; but is every day answered in boy fashion, by idleness, folly, and vice. Give it an answer.

The question of value is a very serious one. The boys mind must be got at somehow or other.

That is the first thing. The teacher ought to be perfectly master of the whole question, and not merely in a vague way deal in general terms, and ipse dixits; if indeed under such circumstances it ever crosses his mind to say anything at all to the boys on the subject. But he ought especially, and before all things, to have some of the elementary truths about the work at his fingers ends; and to be able to drill a hole in a dull mind by a sharp, quick question, " why he is not hoeing turnips, or bird-keeping, earning 35. 6d. a week instead of wasting life and money in school? " and he ought to be able to answer his own question, and send a ray of light in through the hole he has drilled; or rather pull the answer out of the boy himself by a little dexterous manipulation. There are many common facts all round of this kind, which are startling enough, when attention is drawn to their real significance.

The boys of a class were once not a little discomfited, and amused, by something like the following dialogue.

Master. Did you ever hear of Fortunatuss purse?

Boys (two or three). Oh yes, it always had money in it.

M. Would you like to have one?

B. I should just think so, rather.

M. Why dont you get one?

B. Oh, its only a Fairy-story; dont I wish I could?

70 Fortunatus s purse.

M. What! you dont mean to say you dont believe it?

B. Of course not. Who believes in Fairy-stories?

M. I do: really now dont you know where the purse hangs?

B. (quite puzzled). No.

M. Fairy-purses hang on the Fairy-tree to be sure; I have one.

B. (incredulous). You dont say so?

M. But I do (pulling out a shilling); that came from it.

B. (very much taken aback). Are you serious?

M. Quite serious. Where did this shilling come from?

B. Oh, its yours.

M. No doubt. I did not steal it, I hope, but how did it become mine?

B. Oh, I suppose you were paid for keeping school.

M. Well, why dont you keep school? You told me you would like some money.

B. I cant.

M. Why not?

B. I dont know enough.

M. Oh! but what has that to do with it?

B. Of course you must have knowledge to keep a school.

M. Indeed!! Do you mean to tell me that my knowledge turned into money?

B. Yes.

M. What!? This shilling part of a Greek-verb?

B. (laughing). I suppose so.

School fairy-land. 71

M. What are you, pray, doing here?
B. Oh! we come to learn.
M. Not to get knowledge? surely?
B. Of course we do though.
M. You dont mean to say you are climbing the tree of knowledge?
B. (twinkling somewhat). Well I I suppose so.
M. To go back; where does the Fairy-tree grow?
B. (promptly). In Fairy-land, to be sure.
M. You forget. I said I had climbed it.
B. (dubiously). No I dont. Is it the tree of knowledge?
M. Where did my shilling come from?
B. From the knowledge you have.
M. But where does the Fairy-purse hang?
B. You told me on the Fairy-tree.
M. But the shilling came from the Fairy-purse.
B. O-o-h-h!!
M. And you agreed that the Fairy-purse hangs on the Fairy-tree. Now, what is the Fairy-tree?
B. It is the tree of knowledge.
M. And you told me that the Fairy-tree of course grew–in?
B. O-o-h-h-h! Fairy-land.
M. And Fairy-land is?
B. (many broad grins). School.

No Pantomime ever made a more unexpected transformation scene than this, when the whole class with a delighted chuckle perceived that they had been trapped into calling school, Fairy-Land. For a time at all events they did not envy the chimney-sweep.

72 Real value, market value.

No doubt this is but a small part, and a mean part of the subject: nevertheless it is a part, and a necessary-part, and like all beginnings worth notice, and important to beginners. Great confusion appears to exist on the simple point of the value of knowledge, and mental skill. To judge by the opinions generally expressed our friend Will othe Wisp is lord paramount here also, and it is a mere matter of fancy, or chance, or guess work, or individual circumstances, what the value of mental training is. It is quite fleeting, and misty, and immeasurable, and incalculable. Whereas nothing is more definite; nothing more easy to calculate on principle.

It is assumed that the work is being done in the right way. Pump-work is out of the question, even if it fills the kettle. The true value of all true skill is the subject now to be dealt with. The value of all mind work, all work, that is, which requires teaching, divides at once, and falls under two heads: real value; that is, the value of the acquisition to the man himself in himself: and market value; which requires that the acquisition, whether really valuable or not, shall be capable of being bought and sold, and can find purchasers in sufficient numbers. First let it be observed that the number of purchasers is quite distinct from the price at which a given article can be produced so as to yield a profit on its production, and may be dismissed from this investigation;

since it may be assumed that the worker either expects to find purchasers for his work; or, if not, has some other object than a saleable article in view. The actual value of the marketable article, if it is to be sold at a profit, is the question now under consideration; and

The labourer s value. 73 the variation of price produced by the supply exceeding or falling short of the demand does not affect the argument; whilst it tends to create great confusion by introducing a disturbing element of no importance in the first instance. Now the market value of anything and everything which finds purchasers is made up of three factors, the time employed in the producing it, the strength needed in the production, and the risk of failure. The value then, or, in common words, the price at which an article can be brought into the market, is made up of time, strength, and risk. And a mans value is the money interest he can get in the market of the world for these three. By time is meant the number of un-remunerative years which must be spent in learning the skill necessary; by strength, the amount of physical force, or brain-power, or capital, or connexion, or plant, whether material plant, or trade facilities and means of working already gained; and by risk, the uncertainty whether the individual after all his labour and expenditure will succeed; the chance that all may be thrown away, which in many instances cannot be gauged beforehand. All these require to be taken into account in determining value. For example. The farm labourer can begin his work at once. No outlay of unprofitable time is required; his profit begins with his work. No outlay of unusual strength is required; physical strength alone of an average kind is all that is wanted. He runs no risk of failure, as every one can do the work. He earns money as a child, and begins to maintain himself from the first moment that he begins to work at all. These facts decide that a labourers wages will be low.

74 The artizaris value.

No time is lost in being taught. No special strength is needed. There is no risk of failure. No interest therefore has to be paid under any of these heads. Accordingly, though the work itself is the most necessary in the world, in fact the work by which man lives, the payment for the work is low. This is no arbitrary valuation but a law of nature.

But an artizan, a carpenter, let us say, has to acquire skill. He cannot begin earning something at once. He must spend some years before he gets a penny; during all those years he must live, and pay moreover for being taught; and when he does begin on his own account, he has, first, to spend some money in material, and tools, and a working-place; and secondly, to sell his goods, and run the risk of not finding a sale. Interest must be paid on all this, or the work is not worth doing. Skilled work contains these factors of time, strength, and risk, the moment it begins to be skilled work. The artizans work therefore is paid at a much higher rate than the labourers. His wages represent the interest on the time, and brain, he has employed, and they rise in proportion to the amount of these. This is no arbitrary valuation, but a law of nature. Moreover when the additional element of plant, material plant, or other large outlay of capital, involving great and accurate brain power, and much risk, comes in also, then great profits are made, as they deserve to be, by successful men. The most acute underling may turn out a miserable manager. Nothing but trial can show who has the stedfast will that can judge and decide, as well as the sharp eye that can see; nothing but trial can show who will, or will not, succeed

The barrister s value. 75 under the weight of responsibility, and the wear and tear of being the anxious centre to which all the evil and difficulty comes, and the need of being in character, disposition, and firmness, able to make inferiors do well. It is a law of nature therefore that such strength should be paid high.

To proceed another step. A barrister has to spend thirty years perhaps before he earns anything. During all that time his outlay on education and living has been great. He has to face in many instances the risk of not getting work; and in all instances the risk of not being able to do it successfully. For the skill required is of a high order, and cannot be tested with any certainty beforehand; and the chance of failure is proportionate. A barrister therefore, if successful, requires interest on all this expenditure of time, and strength of brain, and risk, and gets it. It is a law of nature that he should do so.

The case of a curate, or of any man who is forced to spend twenty-two and twenty-three years or more in preparation before he can earn a penny, is analogous. It is true in many instances, the interest is not paid; and they do not receive the value of their work, though it is really worth it. Every nation is heavily in debt to its highest workers. For the highest work both in the religious and intellectual world will always be somewhat beyond the range of the intelligence of the majority, and accordingly will be illpaid. A nations rank in the world may always be estimated as high, or low, by the amount it allows itself to be in debt to the higher kinds of work. The fact however that the buyers do not know their own interest in no way affects the true value of the work offered.

76 Mean demand mean supply.

That is determined infallibly by the price of preparation; and that is fixed by time, strength, and risk. The actual money value of the highest education in the market will always be great; inasmuch as powerful minds, able to turn their powers to anything they are required to do, must always be in demand. What they turn their mind to will however depend very much on the demand. A mean demand is met by a mean supply. Able men as a class will go where their abilities are recognised and rewarded. The exceptional case of the religious service is not forgotten. But even there the natural law works incessantly, and a nation alive to the moral welfare of its citizens will appreciate and pay for the work done, in proportion to its capacity to understand it. This holds good in schools also. If the nation wants able men to deal with their children, it must pay for ability. If it thinks that because children are young, they are low-priced, rating their value as a calf, or a sheep, by their age, then the parents will be satisfied with low-priced workmen, and the supply will equal the demand. A shibboleth which to many minds confers plenary absolution, whatever the consequences may be of a wrong demand. Men may demand what they please, but it is a law P ropta"fii,tha t: the highest education must always be capital, involving great 1?. Price is Paid or not-If the much risk, comes in also, thtes elsewhere, or is starved they deserve to be, by successful tne loser-underling may turn out a miserabtt of the money ques-but trial can show who has the s teacher and taught, judge and decide, as well as the sbiife-nothing but trial can show who vour, portable work, as

Beggars rich or poor. 77 truly representing labour as a sack of corn does. And labour is the product of life, life converted into a durable form, capable of being stored, exchanged, transferred, but nevertheless everywhere and always nothing but life in spite of the change of shape. Many have to spend twenty, twenty-five, thirty years of their own lives before they earn a penny for their own support. During all this long period they must live, and they must pay both for living, and for the instruction in skilled work which they are receiving. Where does all this stored-up labour and life come from, which is thus lavished on them, and their education? It is other mens labour, other mens life, the sweat of their brows, and the blood of their hearts, which gives the young the opportunity of thus living and learning. How many hours of labour, and mental pain, and care, and weariness are embodied in those unfeeling coins that maintain the schoolboy in his place of vantage? It is all given in trust. There is an implied contract that work shall be done for it. Work can only be repaid by work. And no beggar who creeps through the street living on alms, and wasting them, is baser than those, who idly squander at school, or afterwards, these lives received on trust, the piled-up life of others, which they have spent or are spending as they live. It is a mean thing to live on alms, and do nothing; be the alms a princely fortune inherited, or a beggars crust; both are equally the stored-up life of other men. And no man has a right to take the stored-up life of others, and pour it out in folly and idleness, at any time or in any place. If this truth was well known to the schoolboy, and part of his stock in trade before he came to school, many a 78 In the name of the prophet, "Jigs."

good, but thoughtless boy would alter his way of going on, and raise the whole work to a much higher level of efficiency by a better appreciation of it.

Money value from this point of view plays an important part in education, and no one is too young to have this truth laid down as a foundation to stand on.

To resume. The market price of the educated man is a necessary factor in education. Only those who have exceptional advantages of stored-up life at their disposal to support them over a term of unpaid years can afford the time, or face the risk, involved in acquiring the skill necessary for even the higher forms of bread-winning. And interest must obviously be paid on this outlay if the public are to reap any advantage from it. Most assuredly the despotism of a mob will no more get work done for nothing, than the despotism of a despot. Valuable work must be paid for, or it will not be done. But it must not be forgotten in dealing with the market price of education, that this by no means represents its real value. Power in a mans self has been proved to be the true object to strive after. And many of the lower forms of bread-winning do not touch this at all, although the possession of inward power touches them. However necessary the consideration of market value may be, and up to a certain point it is necessary, if this were all there could be some excuse for the idle and the ignorant. If education is nothing more than producing the most saleable article in the human market, and realising the greatest profits, then the boy slave, who is being worked up for sale, may fairly have his own idea as to whether the result to be attained is worth the price he is paying

The auctioneer s hammer. 79 for it. The grand doctrine of " every man for sale, in the name of the prophet, figs" will at all times fall rather flat on youthful ears. Is he to sit and toil day by day, and let the sun shine upon hill and dale, and he not see it? and let it gleam along the rivers, and glance in and out of the forest trees with scattered joyousness, and he not see it? Is he to miss the freshness of the air, the games, and the thousand and one delights that pass glittering through the kaleidoscope of the boy mind, so fertile in fancy, so free? And all for what? On the chance, forsooth, that by and by, if he is lucky, he may fetch a high price in the worlds auction room. Is he to strain, and strive, and use time, and energy, and brain, and starve his ravening for free enjoyment and activity and fun, only to put himself up to the highest bidder, and value his life by what other people think of it, and not by what it is worth to himself? This will not do. A thousand reasons, and tens of thousands of excuses, any one of them convincing to a mind so ready to be convinced, bid him answer boldly "no:" and "no" he does answer in practice, a final, invincible "no." Education, if it is to be a prevailing power, must be something which the auctioneers hammer cannot fix the value of, something, that the highest bidder cannot buy, a gain in the man himself. The auctioneers view will never command the hearts and lives of the young. " In the name of the prophet–figs–" is not a war-cry to stir the idle pulse, or give the coward nerve, even though the price be great, and the figs, the sweetness of Paradise. They are far off, very far off, to the boy, and the cry is as a voice in a dream, distant and dim. The present is 8o Pot-hunting.

tempting, all cannot win, and high wages are not life. " Figs " have little charm for the eager foot standing on lifes bright threshold with an untried world in front. A better spell must be found to conjure with than this. There is another spell, which many conjure with, and its power over some cannot be denied. It is a louder and fiercer cry, but not more true; though true, high feelings are often marshalled under it; and there is a noble side of human nature of which this parody of truth takes advantage, and reaps the benefit. The appeal to success, Prizes, and Prizewinning, bids fair to be the watchword of the day. But what does this do for the majority, for the non-competing crowd; who nevertheless do not politely die off, and make room; and cannot through modern squeamishness, be killed off, and buried? There they are, and there they insist on remaining. The character of the appeal is noteworthy. About the year 400 A. d. the Goth, and the Vandal, the Viking, and the whole North, Danes, and Saxons, and Jutes, began to pour in on the civilized Roman world, and brought theh battle-axes against all the civilization of the old order. Physical force was let loose, and smashed everything, and a thousand years were used up before the finer and nobler life of the earlier times had reasserted its preeminence, conquered the conquerors, and given birth to Modern Europe. We are accustomed to call this period the Dark Ages. The name is deserved as far as the triumphs of the strong arm and the battle-axe were real and prevailing. Modern Europe scorns the Dark Ages. But is the axe the only weapon? or physical force the only force? In what respect morally does the strong

The swineherds horn. 81 arm differ from the strong head? Both are mere instruments of a power behind both that uses them. And what is a nation doing which calmly stands up and says, "We will only regard in our schools the breeding of the strong head; and we will give all our honour and power to the wielders of strength"? "Glory to the strong. Boys, whet your tusks, rush, rend, tear, win, make yourselves a name, be great." This is but the Vandal over again, and a swineherds call. The worship of force, no doubt, is an idolatry of a more stirring kind than the greed for market price, but only the more deadly on this account. Glory to the strong on the reverse side of the shield is oppression to the weak. The weak are pushed into a corner, and neglected; their natural tendency to shrink from labour is educated into despair, by their being constantly reminded, directly or indirectly, that their labour is no good. All cannot stand in a conspicuous pillory of success. A base preeminence of brutal strength, however full the trough may be of coronets, or pride of place, belongs to but few; and few comparatively in early years are fired by the thought. Alas for the many, alas for the pith, and working fibre of the nation; alas for all the gentler, and finer qualities by which society lives. The rain, and the dew, and the sunlight, and the crops, and grass that covers the hills with minute blades of life-sustaining power innumerable, must be banished from the world; the volcano carries the day. All tender influences, all prevailing, patient, unpretending good may pack and be gone. There is no room for them in the heart of the modern coming world. Blind Samson is to be king; and Hercules Furens next 82 The Darker Age.

heir to the throne. The pride of intellect is to be unchained; and with the break-up of humility, reverence, holiness, and genius the child of love, the Darker Age will set in, to be wondered at in turn in years to come. There is to be no room for the weak. So a conviction is gradually forced on the practical worker that it is useless for the many to strive for individual skill, and they accordingly accept their doom. Utter deadness to the true power of Education is the natural result of this; and produces an impossibility under the present circumstances of its being got. Yet it is an axiom that a system, which takes no count of the weak, is no part of Gods true world. "Gather up the fragments that remain that nothing be lost," is the watchword of Truth for ever. Now on all sides there is but the dull fierceness of mechanic greed and the auctioneers hammer, or the neglected idlers snores, only broken by the hoarse clamour round the trough, and the loud droning of the swineherds horn.

CHAPTER VI.

THE THEORY OF TEACHING.

Real Value. Growing eyes.

The market value of all skilled work has been briefly dealt with; and the plain principles on which it can be calculated pointed out. It has been proved that mental skill is costly, and that the skilled workman must be paid a high price for his skill if the nation is to benefit by it. At the same time it has been assumed, and with truth, that mankind in general will not busy themselves in acquiring skill which is not likely to bring any return; or in other words, that a reasonable hope of a market will always be an important factor in determining the work of the majority. Nevertheless the auctioneers hammer, and the swineherds horn, have been shown to reach but little way, to be very inadequate as motives even where they reach, to be destructive of the welfare of many, and not to touch the main subject at all. Something is needed which the lowest can get and feel the 84 Platos testimony.

gain of, and the highest can never reach beyond; something for all. If this is a true statement the heaping up of knowledge cannot satisfy this demand, and may stand very much in the way of it. Plato has given a standard to refer to, which may serve by an entirely independent experience to introduce in a striking manner another side of the question. He is engaged in arguing for the immortality of the soul, and bringing proof that human life is not bounded by the narrow limits of birth and death. In the course of his argument he makes the following remarkable statement. " The immortality of the soul," he said, " appeared to him to receive decisive proof from the rapidity with which boys leamt. For they seized on knowledge so readily that they seemed to have come from a previous life, and to be picking up again what they knew before, and not learning something new."

What a marvellous testimony this is to the belief of the learners that the education was worth having, and could be got. What a vivid picture it gives of eager listeners with keen, wistful faces hanging on the lips of teachers; and of teachers, who knew their work, and did it. They at all events believed in education for its own sake. They felt it to be their own lives they were dealing with. There was no deluge on the shut kettle going on in that strange Athenian land. No crowds of unwilling cattle driven into the school corral in the foolish early days, which we have improved on so much. There is Platos statement; a clear, unmistakeable, sober fact, though standing out sharp, and bright as the outline of his own Hymettus under the southern sky. How it sparkles with life and light. How rich in promise of

The stone of Sisyphus. 85 freshness, and happy range, and fruitful tracts of joyous mind, joyous in the freedom of its growth, joyous in the breathing healthy bracing air, blowing from regions bountiful and good. What will the English schoolmaster say on the subject? Answer class-rooms from end to end of this land. Answer everyone, whose work lies within the four walls of any room, where the elite of England are under instruction; and the answer shall be–the answer of Sisyphus–of a heavy weight toilsomely forced up hill, and ever coming back again to crush the forcer. There is no upward spring. There is no life stirring for the sake of life. This will be the answer wherever any attempt is made to train each boy. This will be the answer even in speaking of the few, who are eager, the prize-winners. They race for the prize; but they, even they, as a body, do not work from love of the work for its own living sake, and lose half their time from this half-heartedness: even they never enter into the higher realm of thought in many instances. They are satisfied with the swineherds trough, or the not ignoble duty to their homes. This is no hasty assertion, but the result of many years experience of all kinds; made with the full knowledge of the ease with which unpleasant words are misunderstood, or misrepresented, or mutilated, and set up to be demolished by adverse skill. Any master of words can at any time make the worse appear the better cause before a mixed audience; how much more when the unpleasant words are spoken in the face of the strong motives there are to induce many to contradict them. In spite of all this the judgment is fearlessly put forth as incapable of being contra- 86 Greek sunshine, London fog.

dieted, if rightly understood, that the mass of English minds are dead to education, and will none of it; and that the mental atmosphere in which Plato lived and taught, and the atmosphere in which an Englishman lives and teaches, are to one another as the clear Greek sunshine to the densest London fog.

Let the parents of England see to it. It is their concern. If they believe that an eager desire to practise mental athletics, and to be trained in the indoor work of schools, animates their children, not a word more need be said. But if they have their misgivings on this head, then it is worth considering, why what ought to be increase of power, and a constant source of new interest, should be so distasteful; why in fact the schoolboy, who would not give up his power of reading, and writing, which he has learned to value, nevertheless will not budge another inch, and very often does not budge any appreciable distance, during the fourteen or fifteen years he is theoretically being taught; though he learnt one language as a baby, and was made to read and write afterwards without much more expenditure of labour. Surely he would move if he saw, or felt, anything worth moving for. What are the resources of the bird boy in the field? According to the legend, swinging on a gate, and eating fat bacon, this sums up supreme felicity in his case. But the most stolid schoolboy in his dreariest hour pitches his ambition higher than a gate and fat bacon.

There must be something radically wrong in the process which has turned Platos young Athenian into the English schoolboy. The. other side of the question may

New members, ears, eyes. 87 be briefly summed up in one short sentence; Plato was dealing with the minds of his audience; schools deal now with the books they use. Drawing out the powers of living minds is indeed different from packing in dead facts, even when the packing is neatly done. It is time to begin to treat of training as distinct from packing.

A short view of some of the simpler results of training may serve to lead up to the discussion of the main subject, and show the real value of all true education. It has already been pointed out that thought requires material, and that material is gathered by observation, and that observation is trained work. But the way in which observation and training act, and their wondrous magic, like many every day, habitual possessions, passes without notice. Few are aware of the stupendous fact that skilful training as much produces new growth, and new kinds of growth, in mans mental organism, as a gardener produces new growths, and new varieties of plants, in his garden. New additions can be made to a man, quite as real additions as if new members, or senses were given, the seven leagued boots of the story books, the invisible cap, or the ears that hear the grass grow. Story books often hold truths in striking masquerade. The familiar instance of the sportsman shall serve as the first example. He and his town friend take a walk together through the fields, chatting as they go, to all appearance furnished with the same number of ears, eyes, legs, andc.: suddenly the sportsman breaks off with the exclamation, " look, theres a hare sitting." His two-eyed friend stares about, and asks, where? He is told. He cannot see it. He is told again, and again, and 88 The Sportsman s eye.

again, and still he cannot see it. The exact spot is pointed out, still he cannot see it. And if the assertion formed part of a discussion on an intellectual question not capable of being verified by the senses, he neither would see it, nor could be made to see it; but would remain blind, and unconvinced to the end. However, they advance; and when they get closer, up starts the hare, and proves the truth of the sportsmans words. But the remarkable fact of all is, that this unintentional sceptic did physically see the hare the whole time he was stoutly affirming hc did not. Exactly the same image of the field, and the hare in it, was pictured on the retina of both the speakers, the eye in both cases dealt with the same imprint; yet such is the natural magic in the midst of which we move, that, in spite of this certainty, the one seer sees, and the other does not see, and might stand there in the field to the end of time, and still declare, and declare truly, that he did not see the hare. The difference between training and non-training is so great that the actual fact of physical sight ceases to be sight to the untrained eye; or rather that a new faculty of sight is given to the trained eye, and the man endowed with something in himself, from henceforth inseparable from him. Daily experience testifies daily to the unexpected powers that exist in man, but must be called out by training before they are known to exist. Until the training comes, the eye can be so unconscious, so stupid, as actually not to see what it actually does see, as far as the physical fact of sight goes. And sight, which has passed into a proverb for certainty, is shown every moment to be non-existent till trained.

The Painters eye. 89

The same strange exposure of the delusion that sight is sight, and the same strange discovery of new powers, will happen in a higher degree if the sportsman goes into the field with a painter. But this time the sportsman is the victim. To him the field beneath the rich canopy of the autumnal sky, and heavy clouds, with the great September sun, is grey, or yellow, as he may call it. And grey or yellow would be liberally, and unhesitatingly laid on the canvas, if a brush was put in his hands, and a preternatural skill in wielding it for the nonce given him. Then, and not till then, would he discover, with the fatal evidence before his eyes, self-convicted, how utterly false his idea of what he saw had been. Possibly after that he might be open to receive an account of what had really been imprinted on his eye. And he might be induced to believe that the colours on the varied surface of the stubble, under the changeful sky, ranged in subtle gradations, from deep black in the cloud-swept hollows, and heavy shade of trees, up through every tint of shifting harmonies, that earth, sun-light, straw, gloom of tree, or hedge, or passing cloud could supply, till they melted away in purest white where the slant rays just touched the upland with a rim of light. But this is what the painter sees, and the other does not see. Yet the image on the retina of both is the same. All this is capable of demonstrative proof. If it were not so, how much humility, how much faith it would require in the non-seer to believe that he could thus acquire new sight with the same eyes. This difficulty is increased exceedingly when the next step in the series is taken, and mental pictures come under consideration. These are not capable of go The Poefs eye.

being proved by demonstration, the hare cannot be started, the colour cannot be laid on. Yet if a poet goes into the same field, what manifold marvels his mental vision may behold. Bear witness all happy songs of field, and forest, and stream, and hill, that have been, or shall be, sung on earth. Bear witness butterfly, and flower, bird, bee, and every living thing that gladdens earth with life that moves, in all earths changing moods, and which now make melody for evermore in human hearts dwelling in lasting summer of the poets verse. Yet in all cases the image on the retina is the same. The ploughboy sees the same field; the sportsman sees the same field; the painter sees the same field; the poet sees the same field; the actual eyes of all are the same. Compare the ploughboys world, a prison without light, with the poets world. Compare the prison of the walls of flesh with the dark soul within closed round with gloom, cribbed, cabined, and confined, in its unwin-dowed body, with nothing but a lump of bacon in the midst of the gloom, as its highest thought and joy; compare this and the poets inheritance and empire over worlds on worlds. Nay compare it with the feeblest glimmer of the dawn of light in the heart of the unwilling schoolboy; would not the most stolid schoolboy clamour after light? For he would feel a sense of power and pleasure in himself, a new self beginning to live, and would not let go the feeling, and the gain. But this truth holds good through every gradation of progress, whenever each learner with certainty grows new powers through true guidance and teaching, however slowly it may be. Give the certainty, and there will be no more living

The microscope mental lenses. 91 prisons with bacon, or cricket, in the darkness, as the sole relief, flickering like a farthing rushlight, soon to go out in stench. Man moves in an everlasting mystery of unknown life, from which a new truth may flash at any moment, and education trains the loving eye into a working power able to see truth. Even as the microscope has revealed new worlds, so have the mental lenses of the great poets and thinkers done. Beauty beyond all expression in the meanest created things can be seen by the ordinary eye of even ignorant man by looking through a microscope; and unknown infinities of smallness and perfection, which baffle, even when seen, the powers of the mind to grasp, have become visible to common sight. In like manner literature, and true training, creates sight. And the world of common men, generation by generation, may look through the magic glasses of the mind, and gradually become conscious of the same infinity of unsuspected glory in the midst of which we go about our daily tasks, and move; always in it, never aware of its presence, till some trained eye descries it, and makes it its own, and gives it as a gift to ignorant men; or we ourselves in some happy hour light on some fair discovery of hidden thought. Not a leaf waves in the wind; not a drop of dew comes sparkling out of nothing to gem the bladed grass with orbs of light, without telling something to those fitted to receive it. Thought touches thought with quickening spirit and life enriches life with wealth, until ever mounting upwards the mind becomes a kind of new created king, a lord of thought, lord of an endless kingdom full of light and pleasure and power. Give a certainty of advance, and there will be no more hanging 92 The prison walls open.

back. It is possible to conceive a time when the poorest cottage between the four seas shall be a home of life in its truest and best sense; and its inhabitants move with firm step in the great freehold of cultivated mind. The atmosphere of cultivated mind might pervade society to such a degree that the common conversation of mankind with each other should be full of pleasant novelties of knowledge, and much be gained by mere social intercourse, with but few books. Mind is more powerful, when it is the mind bred and fostered by generations of intelligent work, than the world in any way believes. Now and then the half imprisoned semi-ploughboy commonalty are astonished at hearing of botanists like Dick, and naturalists like Edwards t, bringing the trained eye and loving heart of life that can see, into lowly rooms, and from under humble roof-trees sending out a message of interest to all. But even if original searchers will always be rare both amongst high and low, those who can enjoy what others see and show them need not be rare. When time, and teaching, and love have been at work, the prison walls open, and the lord of thought comes out to take possession, the man whose power is in himself finds himself endowed, as he daily grows in power, with new members, new senses, matchless instruments, and begins to range freely through a glorious universe–a voyager on a boundless sea of discovery, gathering fresh glory and fresh delight as he ranges. Nevertheless all this transmuting power is nothing but observation, loving observation pursuing its work with skill, and working

Life of a Scotch Geologist and Botanist, Robert Dick.

t Life of a Scotch Naturalist, Tho. Edwards, by Samuel Smiles.

Stupidity no more. 93 with sleepless strength, because of skill and love. Time, and teaching, and love, these three, can slowly and surely make the eye see, and the mind inspire the eye, and be inspired in turn. The slowest can begin though the swiftest cannot end. Time, teaching, and love, these three, transmute all things when life is at work. There is no incapacity which can prevent observation. And there is no inability to enjoy what observers give. The great writings of all time rightly treated are but lenses which all can look through. The problem of power in a mans self is capable of no hard solution. There is no stupidity. Once impress on the minds of a generation that teaching and training are names of life, and pleasure, names of new senses, new strength, new delights, which all can attain, and Platos schoolboy will appear again. There will be no stupidity.

CHAPTER VII.

THE THEORY OF TEACHING.

Observation. Mental Law. Accuracy.

Observation, or, in other words, intelligent work has been shown to be the be all and the end all of teaching and training. This fact does away with stupidity. The importance of bringing the subject into well-defined limits, and proving it to be within everybodys reach, cannot be overrated. One great consequence at once results from this. Given proper conditions, a teacher is bound to succeed; with its corollary, that, given proper teaching, ignorance is not a misfortune, but a crime. Nevertheless a man cannot till a field by walking up and down it scattering corn. In bringing land under cultivation much has to be done before the sowing begins. This is self-evident. The ground has to be considered, and the state it is in, and how far it needs to be prepared for receiving the seed. In like manner in cultivating mind it is no less self-evident that mind itself must be dealt with. And a glimpse has already been given in the shut kettles and the pumping, of how many things may have to be done before the mind can receive anything. Often

Observation and Accuracy. 95 and often the inspiring a belief in value and in the possibility of getting the object is the necessary preliminary, without which all other application of skill is wasted labour. But a great step is gained when the simple proposition that mind has to be dealt with is accepted. The question is at once brought out of the clouds. The teachers subject is mind; therefore to mind he must first address himself, whatever else he may afterwards betake himself to. The whole matter rests on the best method of awakening, and exercising dormant faculties, of directing, and training them, of giving them material to work on, and finally, of so increasing their vigour, and quickening them into higher life as to amount to nothing less than a giving practically of new senses, and creating as it were a new creature. Now mind is an active, living power, and its energy and working manifestation is thought. Thought then is the teachers care, and the production of thought his intention. But as mind is a living power, with all the changeful properties of life, not only the production of thought, but the training and shaping it in such a way as to become skilful, self-restrained, and consciously harmonious, is a teachers province. The work of a teacher then is twofold, producing thought, and training it. Two familiar words, allowed a fair latitude, will condense all that a teacher has to do. Observation and accuracy, define the whole range. Under the head of observation falls all imparting of new powers, and drawing out the old. And under the head of accuracy falls all skill in arrangement, and all perception and practice of due proportions, by which varied material is put in place, and brought into harmonious use. Let it g6 King Topsy-Turvy.

be noted in passing that memory has no more to do with true power than the cart which carries the seed-corn to the field has to do with the growth of the crops.

It has been shown that thought cannot exist without material to call it forth and exercise it. The material again is twofold; if the same term can rightly be applied to two very different kinds of things. First, there is the material already in the mind unknown, the latent facts, like the hare on the retina of the townsmans eye, where all that is needed is to bring out an existing power. Under this head is grouped all material already gathered unconsciously, as material known to be there, but not heeded as being common, language for instance, the ordinary every-day sights and conditions of the visible world; all this is ready to hand, and ought to be utilized, and lighted up, so far at least as to awaken a sense of an unknown world existing in common things. Secondly, there is the work of acquiring fresh knowledge, and exciting observation by a new and previously unknown class of facts. Of these two the material ready at hand, familiar, and unimpeded by the necessity of mastering, or, alas, not mastering strange symbols, claims attention first, and most. In the first place, there it is. A fact, the importance of which can scarcely be exaggerated. Certainly those who have watched the vast capacity in the boy mind for not having things there, and the curious menagerie in which King Topsy-Turvy reigns supreme over what is supposed to be there, will not be inclined to undervalue what really is there. The learners native language ought to be the groundwork of all teaching. By this is meant the actual language, a skilful examination of

Thought lessons in cricket. 97 the common sentence as a vehicle of intelligent thought, with its structure and necessary requirements; not what is often called teaching English, not the philology, or history, or literature, or curiosities and idioms, but the very common talk we talk, and why, and how, we talk, if we talk correctly, or what follies we commit, if we talk incorrectly. Many pretend that this logical fashioning of grammar is beneath their notice; and fly to one or other of the above-mentioned substitutes, which are very pleasant but if considered to be a training in the English language are delusions. If the real language work is taken the ground is familiar enough, but there are plenty of hares in it to surprise the untrained mind. On the same principle from time to time a lesson in question and answer on some familiar thing should be given. For example, let a teacher give his class a spirited cross-examination on cricket, and why cricket is a favourite game, with the intention of baffling them by Socratic logic, driving them into corners, exposing their ludicrous beliefs, forcing them to arrange their ideas, and disentangle their confused statements. Let him make them clear out why they like it, and discover how much of pain, and difficulty, and disagreeable, there is in what seemed to them a matter of course; and then let him generalise, and push them back on those properties of human nature which, by being called into active exercise, make cricket interesting, as well as many other things besides cricket. All the secret thoughts excited, and the amusing overthrows in argument form no insignificant training, when the teacher brings out what trials the game puts its votaries to, what its real merits are, and at every turn 98 Lessons in chairs.

startles them by some new dilemmas. A hare jumps up at every step, no mean magic is shot into the every-day world; and a sense of their ignorance being insecure, and not such perfect knowledge as they thought, because it was familiar, begins. Tell a class to define a chair, or a room, or an inkstand, or any common object, and in a skilful way refute and ridicule their vague, general terms, and expose the gaps and defects in their statements, and a new ray is dashed across their life, a flash, which however momentary, has cloven the darkness. They have seen, and from henceforth sight cannot quite leave them again. Whilst those who care move with awakened curiosity in a sort of land, where at any moment, as in dreams, or story books, the log of wood may spring up as an enchanted prince, or the toad turn round, and appear as the long-sought bride. A sense that nothing is only what it seems begins to be felt, and a suspicion that everything they see, or do, or touch, has a pleasant trick to play them finds entrance.

The late Dean Dawes, of Hereford, drew attention to the value of calling out observation in common things in an original and striking way. Unhappily the clue he gave towards education in the National Schools has not been followed up. In fact, it was entirely broken off by a different demand on the part of the authorities.

The mere fact of answering questions with thought is a great point gained. Pumped-on boys cannot answer questions.

It is true the power of questioning on common things requires that the questioner shall be a skilled workman, a teacher; but in theory, on paper, it is allowable to

Eyes and eyes. 99 imagine such a being. It is true also that the power to question implies that a class be not too large to be questioned; but in theory, on paper, it is allowable to imagine such a class.

Common things have the priceless advantage of being common, of being there. And as soon as common things have this spark, this fuse, thrown in amongst them, there is no limit to the possible effect. All the world with its startling contrasts and secrets becomes one great lesson book. All the marvels that lie hid even in the dust of our feet may at any moment quicken into fairy births. At least the distinction is seen between the unthinking and the intelligent eye, between the familiarity that breeds contempt, because it is ignorant, and the familiarity that brings the worshipper on his knees because he has been brought near to greatness, and can see it, which tends to remove the reproach that clings to the mean man for ever of not being able to know the prophet. The prophet can be known if the mean man is made intelligent. The hero will be a hero to his valet, if the valet is given the eye to see heroes. This process of drawing attention to the unknown known, and exciting interest by awakening new power, is of universal application, and can be applied to new material to lighten the labour of gathering it in, as well as to the old. Two examples shall be given in illustration of this fact, which shall be taken from the least promising area of drudgery. Few are aware, when a little boy is groaning over his Latin with about the same feeling of relationship to it as to " Anthropophagi, and men whose heads do grow beneath their shoulders" that from eighty to ninety per ioo Magic transformations.

cent. of the main words, which occur in a Latin author, are found in English also, and are always skipping in and out over his own tongue; and that instead of being a strange novelty, a kind of wild beast, the hateful apparition is only English in an old coat, a toga, and a tame domestic creature enough. But what a light this kind of fact may be made, at the same time that it not only takes the weight off, but also fastens the work on to things already known. Those known things moreover are discovered to have new properties and a fresh interest; they open, as a door might open into a garden, and disclose an interior view with flowery space, where before there was a blank wall

Another of the great schoolboy wild beasts disappears at a word in the same manner, the difficulty arising from the numerous changes in the endings of words. This will be dealt with further on. But one thing may be noted here, that all these variations are only badges which, like the address on a parcel, tell where each word ought to go. Many magic transformations of this kind exist, which teachers will readily find for themselves. The pleasurable surprise of disentangling the confused skein of boy ideas, and making them see how much they really know, and what they really think, and why, is a never-failing source of interest in good teaching. From all this it will be seen that the beginning of teaching consists in rousing some intelligent appreciation of what is already known by rote, or daily seen by eyes that see not, and daily done without understanding, and despised, because not understood. Attention ought to be drawn to the innumerable links between common familiar objects and

Training and non-training. 101 the new bits of learning, and the whole structure of mind-work made one organism in this way, and one life breathed into it all.

This slight sketch of the first duty of a teacher to excite observation will serve as an outline for work, and indicate the direction of the path. Not least it will point out clearly that there is a path. If the distinctive character of training as opposed to non-training can also be found, and laid down with any precision, then the main roads into the great empire will have been marked out, and the wilderness character of the work got rid of both in imagination, and in fact.

The distinctive character of Training can be found by seeing what characteristic is common to all examples of skilled work. To begin with physical skill. Put a rifle into the hand of the keenest eye, and steadiest strength, in the world (strength and keenness of sight shall be conceded for arguments sake), bid him fire at a mark, and he will miss; though a very moderate rifleman shall hit it. The difference lies in the power of the trained man, however inferior naturally, to send the bullet accurately to the mark he wishes to hit. Put an axe into the hand of the most active athlete, and bid him cut down a tree. His blows will fall with laughable eccentricity anywhere but in the right place, in spite of his activity and strength. But a very poor creature, who has been accustomed to handle an axe, will deliver every stroke to within a hairs breadth, and accomplish the work with ease. The trained hand is accurate. Bid anyone who is not a botanist, describe a plant. The failure even of very educated minds is ludicrous. He IO2 The beginning and the end.

will say it is green, or prickly, or this, or that, terms equally applicable to a lizard, or a hedgehog, to say nothing of a legion of other plants. But a botanist will at once name a score of little typical facts of leaf, and tendril, and stem, and flower, which mark distinctly what the plant is, and separate it from any other plant. Training has first made him observe accurately, and then invent words to express accurately what he has observed. And so on, through all instances of skilled labour, the excellence common to all trained workers is accuracy. Accurate observation of little things marks the accurate observer. Accurate observation of very little things marks the very accurate observer. The very accurate observer becomes the master of many facts old and new: the master of many facts old and new, each in its place, has all that teaching can do to make him a great man.

Training means accuracy. Observation and accuracy are twins. The beginning of all true work is accurate observation, the end and crown of all true work is an accuracy which observes everything, and lets nothing escape, a power of observation animated by a true love for what it undertakes to investigate, and able through love to discover subtler truth than other people. Observation and accuracy comprise all that it is possible for a teacher to do, whatever may be the subject with which he has to deal. And observation and accuracy ought first to be as the joy of the explorer to the curious child; who should be made to see in every word he speaks, and every common thing he sets eyes on endless surprises, and novelties at every turn of unexpected pleasure, and new delight.

CHAPTER VIII.

THE THEORY OF TEACHING.

The Schoolboys Briar-patch, Latin and Greek.

An exercise ground is wanted for the drawing out, and practice of thought, observation, and accuracy. For though the whole world is their practice ground, and the better the surface facts of the world are known the better do they lend themselves to research and further knowledge, yet it is necessary to have a fixed course for teaching, and necessary to utilise the experience of past generations. These two necessities are very important. A common subject, and an old subject is required. The theory of teaching indeed can employ any subject; but as teaching is a practical science it must be illustrated by practice. The choice of the illustration will depend on what is the highest subject of mental training accessible to all, and in commonest use; inasmuch as the highest IO4 Wanted, a practising ground.

subject of mental training in commonest use appeals to the experience of the greatest number, both in present and past time. There must be such a subject from the nature of things. And the Theory and Practice of teaching must take that subject as its illustration. There is no choice. Other subjects, however excellent, or important, have little or nothing to do with illustrating the general principles of teaching from lack of range, or lack of common use. The study of language is such a subject. First of all the study of the students own language. The fact that the English language is not the first training of the English nation, and that no Englishman is taught a thorough mastery of how to speak, and put out thought in his own language, at once puts English education on a very low level. Next to the learners native language comes the great fact that the literary education of the world, that is, the education of higher thought and its expression, has been based for two thousand years on the study of Greek and Latin. Nothing else covers so wide a space in time, or exercises mind to the same extent. Yet from various reasons the power of Greek and Latin as mental training is not understood, and as long as memory is chiefly employed never will be understood. As exercises of memoiy they are bad. The schoolboy especially does not understand what he is about. It is a perfect wilderness to him. But he ought to understand what he is about. The schoolboys wilderness now claims our attention as no wilderness, but the home of culture. Many a schoolboys idea of school and education is vague in the extreme as to the benefit, and vivid in the extreme as to the discomfort. They

The Schoolboys wilderness. 105 find themselves thrown, into a perfect thicket of new tormenting words in strange languages, every word bristling with little thorns, and every little thorn specially provided for them, so it seems, in a prim artificial region from which it is the fondest wish of their hearts to escape as soon as possible, and join the ranks of their elders, who roam outside the tangled brambly plot in flowery space, or at least, flowers or no flowers, unmolested by the peculiar boy-privilege of prickles. They get but little knowledge; most assuredly knowledge would come to them far more easily in their own language. What is it all worth? Is there any meaning in the briar-patch? These are very natural questions, and the beginner, who most probably has been told, if he has been told anything, to gain knowledge, has no chance of answering them without help, which he does not get. Nevertheless, if observation and the observant eye are precious, and training gives them; if accuracy is the result of training; and training in observation and in accuracy is the true work of the teacher and learner, then there is meaning in the briar-patch.

Two things are necessary in training mind. There must be something to call mind into play; and there must be teaching skill to enable the mind to profit by its exercise. That is to say, there must be a familiar subject rich in intelligent difficulties; and there must be intelligent skill to turn those difficulties to account. To give an example. Let Map-knowledge be put forward as a desirable subject to know. Everybody will at once admit that it is desirable. But let Map-knowledge be put forward as an efficient subject for training mind. First io6 Inventories do not train.

of all the boy operated on has no Map-knowledge in him; Maps are not a part of his mind; and secondly, Map-knowledge is a mere inventory of facts, and like any other inventory can be made an effort of memory, and never require any exercise of mind whatever. This dropping in of dry knowledge instead of calling out and strengthening living power is no training of mind. No memory-work is true mind-work. A great demand on the memory convicts a subject of being low in educational value. Let no one suppose that the teaching of geography as it can be taught is undervalued by what has been said. Map-knowledge and nothing more, is not the study of the wonders of earth, and sea, and climate, and all the marvels which may belong to geography. Contrast then the inventory work with thought, language, and literature, the difference is seen at once. The first is from outside dropped in. What is dropped in can be dropped out again. The second is from inside strengthened. Strength within remains. The demand is for an exercise ground for mind. If besides this, wonderful gains are the result so much the better; and it must be something common to all. Mankind require in the first instance something perfectly well known as material for thought, and yet full of unknown problems for the exercise of the mind. The imagination may run riot in paradoxes to describe what is wanted, and yet find all its paradoxes sober realities in the subject found. Something is required which shall be perfectly easy, and at the same time perfectly hard; familiar to all, and known to none; of universal use, and universally strange to the users; so simple, that babies learn it with ease, so com-

Language preeminent. 107 plicated, that the ablest are ever learning it unsuccessfully; the most fixed of all things, and the most shifting; plain, yet infinitely obscure; the common property of ignorance and wisdom; the joint inheritance of the ploughboyand the poet; holding nothing, and yet full of all things; all these, and many more like paradoxes are reconciled in language. Language is the material ready at hand for the training of the whole world. Language is the most perfect field of exercise for accuracy, at the same time that it is the mistress of all knowledge, and the medium of all thought. It combines the greatest artistic skill for making the skilled workman, with the greatest amount of furniture for stocking his shop. The whole world, as it emerges from the nursery, has already gained without conscious labour the best material, as has been previously shown. No nation can be considered therefore to have made a beginning of true educational system, which does not use the store of material, which the most ignorant have already got, in order to train thought, observation, and accuracy. The English language is preeminently qualified to draw out, and exercise thought in a systematic and accurate manner, inasmuch as there are but few inflexions and word badges, so both teacher and learner are forced to consider each word in each sentence on its own merits, to think about it, and assign its grammatical value by thought, instead of having much of the grammar work already done for them by the terminations of the words. This prevents a pernicious exercise of memory from being mistaken for true knowledge. Perhaps also this necessity is the explanation why no one teaches it. But all training ought to io8 Comparison of language.

begin with a quiet mastery of the sentence, the value of each word grammatically, the grammatical value of each term, and each clause, their necessary connexion, and the way in which the whole is built up, thoroughly gone through and elucidated in the native language of the learner. This is the first step. As soon as the laws of thought passing into language have been mastered; and those universal necessities of speech spoken to communicate thought have been known, which belong equally to every language in the whole world, and which are exceedingly simple in principle, and readily understood, when clearly stated, before the mind has become clogged with mistakes,–then comparison of language ought to begin. In other words a strange language should be learnt in order to give scope for a greater experience; and to show how the same laws under different conditions produce exceedingly different apparent results, which nevertheless are a true embodiment of the principles.

We are now coming to the schoolboys briar-patch; the Latin and the Greek,–with all their vexatious, useless trials,–before any real grasp of the literature and life contained in them comes. As few comparatively arrive at any real application of their literary excellence, if it is right to base all higher education on these languages, their claim must rest on something different from mere excellence as literature, or they are unfitted for the training of the many. No stress therefore will be laid on their literary merits here. Though it is fair to mention some of them, lest silence should be mistaken for not having anything to say, when it only means that there is no room to say it, and that it is somewhat beside the

Latin and Greek. 109 present purpose. No one however will lightly pass by the fact, that Latin and Greek are the foundation of much of the spoken language of Modern Europe, our own included, of all modern literary knowledge, and are the only access to the history of the progress of the human race, the only realm in which mans intellectual greatness can be adequately studied. They are the consummate master-pieces of artistic skill and beauty of form, strange talismans to call up spirits with, grand mausoleums of past glory, marvellous museums of early genius, very practical workshops, which might save modern workers from repeating old mistakes and exploded experiments, numbers of which the clever ignorance of each generation puts out again, the regular stock-in-trade of the shrewd, brand-new politician, who always thinks he has discovered perpetual motion, always is ready with a new pair of hinges for the world. It is curious to observe also the strange violations of artistic laws committed constantly by really eminent men, which could scarcely occur if classical composition, and ancient works of art had been familiar; mistakes which arise sometimes from neglecting well-known rules, sometimes from an ab urd imitation of what is admired, but not understood. No sane person thinks himself a poet because he writes good Greek Iambics; or puts them forth as poetry; and whenever the world is sane, men will cease to regard works of art of any other kind as higher than good schoolboy exercises, when they merely reflect the ideas of old time. The idolatry of models marks a child epoch in any works of mind. But the classical models are models of external grace in all subjects which no Old material and new.

the ancient could undertake. A book might be written on every one of the headings just recited; any number of books indeed, but the whole of this side of the question must be excluded, as only partially belonging to school work, and utterly incapable of being dealt with in a small space; yet if the first steps to this great higher world of thought-power were taken away from the many, numbers who now enjoy the benefit would never have had a chance given them of doing so; and some of the very best would have been left out altogether. A nation need think long and well before it cuts away the first rungs of the great thought-ladder from under the feet of its upper classes.

To resume. The study of Greek and Latin simply as a matter of training for the many presents itself as a very important fact; part of which shall now be considered. At first sight there is a great gap between the learner with his own native language, and the learner with Latin and Greek given him as his work. There appears no slight contradiction between strong advice to take advantage of material ready to hand, and immediately after strong advice to begin to master the strangest and most difficult of new material. This contradiction is heightened when the intermediate subject of modern languages is thrust in; and a vigorous claim made on their behalf as logically, and in practice, the thing needed. There is however no contradiction whatever. It is roughly the difference between teaching a lad to ride on a quiet horse, and as soon as he can ride mounting him on a hunter and sending him across country; nothing more. The common principles of sentence-structure, and uni-

Elaborate parrots not wanted. 111 versal grammar are best learnt in the learners own language. After that all fair difficulties become an advantage, not a disadvantage. Observation and accuracy have been laid down as the work of teaching. Observation requires novelty, and accuracy requires difficulty for practice.

So the stupendous advantage of their not being spoken languages, shall be boldly put forward as the most prominent merit of Latin and Greek. No words can exaggerate the importance of this fact. It renders it at once impossible to substitute the glibness of an elaborate parrot, and an infantile familiarity with the sounds, for a real knowledge of the language. In other words, the language cannot be learnt by imitation, as by a baby in the nursery, who acquires a very useful, and necessary faculty of speaking, which no one undervalues; but acquires it without the slightest mental training, and cannot in any sense be said to have received any education by this exercise of memory. A few words on memory will not be out of place here, as no subject perhaps is more misunderstood, and the misunderstandings arising from ignorance on this point affect seriously both the practice and the objects of learning.

Nothing shows more conclusively how poor a faculty mere memory is, and how utterly the part it plays in education is secondary, and how easily it may be overrated, than the curious fact that the greatest feat of memory most persons ever perform in their lives is baby work, done in the nursery. The infant in the nursery during the first three or four years of his life, sucks in, as it were, a language, acquires a considerable vocabulary, ii2 Baby work not wanted.

and, stranger still, the various uses of words implied in the structure of sentences, which every child who talks fluently finds no difficulty in putting together. It is obvious that if the untrained baby mind can perform this feat, without being trained in the least by doing it, that the excluding this disturbing element of the parrot from the main subjects of training is a priceless gain. Hence a modern spoken language, which may easily be nothing but a mere repetition of the baby, and must always be so in some degree, is put out of court at once as a valuable training subject for the young. And all work, in like manner which is memory work only, a heaping in of crude material, however valuable it may be, and, however much, from various reasons, parents, masters, and pupils may stick to it, is unworthy the name of education, and, if much valued, is a most injurious idolatry. This mechanical collection of material by a sort of instinct is however very different in kind from the intelligent production of strong impressions, as Dr Pick has well pointed out, and must not be confounded with it. Triumphs of mere memory it has been shown, are not only no proof of ability, but very often stand exceedingly in the way of training, and tend to destroy it. Accordingly Latin and Greek, as far as they exclude this delusive sham, are fitter subjects for education than anything that does not do so. The necessity of turning the mind however feebly on to the words and sentences to be dealt with, instead of soaking them in by a repeated hearing, forms one great reason for choosing them

Lecturer on Memory, 18 Queens Road, London.

Grammar made visible. 113 to train the many. Their strangeness is their merit. The very facts vulgarly urged against their study turn out to be the very chief reason for studying them. Again, as both these languages are strongly inflected, a necessity at once arises of attending to a number of small changes of form with corresponding change of sense, constantly recurring, and proceeding on a most orderly plan, so that again, and again, in every sentence the same peculiarities make their appearance with the same effect; and the grammar work when these are once mastered, is to a great extent done ready to hand. The eye, without any further examination, sees the grammar. These changes, like the shapes of the leaves to the botanist, require observation, but once observed, tell their own story, and make everything fall into its proper place, and become intelligible. This demand for observation in a thousand ways calls on the loose, slack, happy-go-lucky boy-mind to tighten up, get sinew, and fasten resolutely on them; at the same time that, if he does so, they satisfy the learners feeling, and reward him by the greater ease and clearness of the work. All the little briars and vexations of the old word-empire are like the hedge round the enchanted princess in the fairy tale; they torture and slay the dawdler; he sticks amongst them, and never gets through; but they open of their own accord to the earnest challenger. Vexatious as they appeared at first sight they are just the supreme excellence by which these languages train mind, force it to be accurate, and make it see the beauty of order. This last point is important. If thought at once touched thought all men would put out the thoughts that moved them most strongly 114 Thoughts and labels.

first, and the rest in order of strength. But thought does not touch thought. Words have to be employed, and words come out one by one, and must grammatically, that is, by the laws of words, come in particular order. That order is determined, if the words determine it, by the necessity that the words should fit together, whether they are important or unimportant, so as to deliver their message coherently; but if the thoughts determine it, by the vividness of the thoughts. These two principles do not agree. Thought like a bird would fly straight to its mark, but words compel it to go by very round-about roads. The ancient languages got over much of this difficulty by labelling, as it were, every word, ticketing it with its proper value and sense, by changing the last syllable, or more. In this manner, as long as too great liberties are not taken, or words of the same ending do not clash, much greater variety of arrangement becomes possible, and the forcible part of the thought can be put first in the sentence, though its grammatical place may be last, without creating any confusion, because no one can mistake it for anything else.

This facility is readily illustrated by figures. Let us suppose that the figures go together by pairs. Let i, i, 2 2 3t 3 be taken, it does not matter in the least how they are arranged; as far as the meaning of each figure is concerned 3 is 3 whether it comes first, or last, and the eye sees at once the twin 3 which belongs to it. But take on the same plan n, n, n, then if these pairs are by theory different, unless they follow one another servilely in order of place, no one can tell which ought 4 oair with which, and inextricable confusion is the re-

Order in disorder. 115 suit. It follows from this that an inflected language has great power of varying the arrangement of its words according to the strength of the thought. Hence arises the entirely strange order of the Latin, or Greek sentence, which is so puzzling to a beginner, but which, when once understood, adds so much to the interest of the work, and not unfrequently to the clearness of it, and in consequence to the ease with which it can be done. What a field for thought and observation is opened by this new power. The learner is led to compare the two ways of expression, to examine the real value of the thought intended, to see which of the two languages has succeeded in bringing out the true meaning best, and why it is best. Even a beginner can be made to see that he cannot put the sense of one language into another, until he has found out the sense; and the true sense is often different from the apparent sense as a chestnut horse a horse-chestnut. No Englishman who only knows knguage is in the least aware how very seldom n lish correctly expresses the real meaning ue conveyed; as many a boy has found to, v/st, who has hammered English into Latin words regardless whether he had found out the true sense of the English or not. The English language is full of power, and full of feeling, and produces its great effects

Compare, 3 2i231

Corripit en subita trepidus formidine ferrum 32i231,

II 223 3 isudden

112233.

with./Eneas troubled with sudden fear seizes his sword, n6 Muddle and knavery.

by the use of very pregnant epithets, and strong substantives, which teem with undefined vigour and life. The Latin language is intensely logical, and precise. Two more opposite instruments for the expression of thought cannot be imagined. The moment the subtle Latin probe comes to be applied to the English sentence, the discovering the exact sense contained in the forcible, inaccurate English words becomes a most curious exercise of mind. It is no answer to this statement to say it is not done. No one knows better than the writer that in the empire of King Topsy-Turvy, and his rote work, nothing of the kind can be done. There is no time for it, and no one to teach it; but nevertheless it is one of the principal facts of language-study, and it ought to be done. As long as the great majority of educated people do not know the precise meaning of their own language, when they use it, the confusion and muddle in public and private life must be as great as it is. A man who knows the real meaning of his own words will not use them ambiguously unless he is a knave; and if he is a knave, an audience accustomed to study thought in its processes of taking shape in words will detect his knavery. At present words have absurd power because they are swallowed whole. But a generation trained carefully to find out the precise thought embedded in an English sentence, with its arrangement according to grammar, and not according to force of meaning, and accustomed to rearrange it carefully in the clearest and most forcible way, according to strength of meaning, and not according to the demands of the grammar, would come to their work with a different kind of mind. The anatomical

Sentence-anatomy. 117 study of thought embodied in language can scarcely be pursued with any great success in one language only, and the Latin and the Greek languages are the most perfect means for teaching this science. All the more effectual because our own native tongue is so utterly different in its way of treating thought that observation is roused by every sentence; and observation and accuracy are the natural consequence of any true system of teaching the ancient masterpieces of the expression of thought. The pulling sentences to pieces in order to find out the different ways employed by different languages in producing the same thought to the world is work which even a beginner is capable of doing, and profiting by, in no slight degree. Later on, as soon as a little progress is made, the exquisite beauty of words set in perfect shape, as the beautiful dress of noble thought, begins to be discerned. The fascination of clear-cut, crystalline speech, reflecting and embodying feeling, and life, and delicate perceptions of mind, is felt. None can tell why, but none, who has ever seen it, can forget the charm, the magic charm, of perfect words. In this way the learner grows a new sense, and advances to the intelligent observation of beauty, until at last the fact comes out that the highest thoughts of the highest minds of the wonderful old world are presented in their highest shape to the minds eye with a tenderness and grace, and symmetry, and harmonious outline, which has never been surpassed, and never will be; for our worship has passed on from the outward glory of form to the inward glory of spirit and life. But this is all the more reason that the artist in words should study these as the artistic study, without n8 Artistic skill.

which no great writer or speaker, however well he may write or speak, can be a conscious master of his art; without which great writers and speakers, the few, that is, who lack this knowledge, frequently betray by blemishes and curious defects, that in spite of their success they want the training, which a better education can give. The world will never know what it has been saved from in the way of outrages on good sense and taste even by the limited knowledge of Greek and Latin authors that the average schoolboy acquires. Though some guess may be made by noting the utterances of the clever ignorant who make themselves conspicuous by their tongues.

This sketch would be too imperfect if it did not bring forward another great fact which will ever put the study of Greek and Latin at the top of educational subjects. The unchanging character of the old languages is a practical advantage of the strongest kind. As being Greek and Latin they are old, as being languages they are eternally young. For more than two thousand years men have been engaged in studying these works; and century after century fresh ability is brought to bear on them, and they are daily put out in more attractive forms; and adapted skilfully for student use. Every new discovery in archaeology throws fresh light on them; every advance in politics and religion throws fresh light on them; and receives fresh light from them; whilst all the time they remain the same. For a thousand years they have been worked in England as the highest form of education; and as the years pass by ingenuity exhausts itself in bringing them out in fresh attire for high and low, for the

Perfect fixity, perfect mobility. 119 learned and the school-boy alike, and ever will continue to do so. For the minds of men will never cease investigating these marvels of mind; and every advance in language knowledge as thought taking a living shape, will cast light backwards on the unsurpassable perfection of the early shapes in which thought was enshrined, the more the growth of life, and its passing into words is studied.

There is then perfect fixity, and perfect mobility in this ancient literature viewed as a training. Perfect fixity, inasmuch as the written word does not change. Perfect mobility, inasmuch as the power of life to interpret life is ever changing, and growing greater. Their fixity enables generation after generation to send them on unchanged in substance, but enriched with every advantage that new discoveries give. Their mobility ensures perpetual novelty; since the nobler the literature of any country may be, the higher the minds engaged in it; the better qualified that country and those minds are to see the old models in new lights, to test their own work by them, and make fresh applications of their principles. Shakespear himself might find his powers taxed to put the ancient beauty of words into words as beautiful of our day: how much more shall the task exercise the busy brains of teachers, however able, to the end of time! There is always something to improve on. The ultimate end of the study of the classics is to make the learner an artist in words, and a conscious master of his own tongue. Though men have been now at work for centuries how much remains to be done in this field. In some respects the study has scarcely yet begun. But long before any artistic skill is called out the early stages are fitted to open the mental 12O The briar-patch bears fruit.

eye, to make it observant, to fix habits of accuracy, and awaken thought. Without saying a word more, (and how much more might be said,) it is evident what a marvellous instrument of training has been provided for these latter days in this ever-fixed, and ever-changeful embodiment of powerful life; and how strangely adapted it is to bring out latent faculties, to perfect the skilled workman, to make him an artist of mind, and save him from the mistakes of untutored strength, and the gewgaws of rank imagination, so that he shall not flaunt himself like a savage in his war paint: whilst the accuracy engendered is no mean power added to the ordinary stuff of ordinary men. The very beginning of skill enables the skilled workman to direct his mind aright, to employ what strength he has without waste, and prevents him from worshipping false types, and being deluded by clever charlatans. These are facts. They are facts moreover which are the outcome of principles of irresistible truth. No fashion however triumphant, no ignorance however powerful, can lower the value of the most skilful expression of thought and mind-power. Man the thinker must always be trained to think by exercising his faculties on the most perfect works of thought. It is no accident but a veritable law of nature that makes the highest language-study rank as the highest training. And though it is quite immaterial to the theory of teaching what subject has to be taught; it is not immaterial what subject is taken as the most perfect illustration of the Theory. Enough has been said to show that language, and Greek, and Latin, are the most perfect practice-ground in the world for training mind. So much for the boys briar-patch.

CHAPTER IX.

THE THEORY OF TEACHING.

The Furniture Shop, and the Skilled Workman.

The kettle, lid on or off, and the pumper, give a very true picture of modern theory and practice. But it is clear from what has been said that pumping in knowledge is not education. Everyone can supply examples where there was much knowledge, and no education. When this is the case, knowledge is not power, and the common axiom is seen to be a fallacy. But if knowledge can thus fail even when it succeeds, how much greater a failure is there when it does not succeed; when knowledge is not gained, and education is not gained, as must always be the case in a vast number of instances, where the pursuit of knowledge is made the main object. The Teacher and the Trainer has to make his pupil strong, and skilful in himself, to direct existing powers, and call new powers into existence. The learner does not want to be made a receptacle of other mens words and thoughts, but to be 122 The knowledge-shop.

made a thinker ot thoughts, and a wielder of words himself. It is true that material must be collected or there can be no thought; and that the thinker, as Aristotle says, must learn to become a skilled workman by working at that in which his skill is afterwards to be shown; so far knowledge is necessary. But it is equally true that the perpetual heaping in of more material is easily pushed to an extent that renders thinking over any of it impossible; just as a man who spent his life in collecting timber in order to do carpenters work would never be a carpenter, though he had stacks on stacks of planks in his timber-yard, no not even if the timber had already been made into furniture by other hands. In fact a shop full of ready-made furniture on the one side, and the skilled workman with his tools, and his skill, on the other, do most accurately express the great distinction between the walking knowledge-shop, and the thinker with power in himself. It is true that few acquire great knowledge without some thought, and also that the thoughts of other people often pass current as the speakers or writers own; but this circumstance will not in any way complicate the question with those who can, and will, look to principles. Mere knowledge is not power; and mere knowledge is not education.

To approach the question from another side; the possession of great knowledge is given but to few. The average of general efficiency is alone worth considering in dealing with what teaching and training can do. Here there neither is, nor can be, any doubt. Workmen are wanted. The work of the world cannot get on without workmen, even the shops cannot exist unless there have

The skilled workman. 123 been skilled workmen. The need of the world at any moment is not wealth, that is, the result of work finished and done; but work, and workers, that is, the living power and skill that continue to produce. Production comes before display, production comes before making up; without the producing power how poor, how impossible, prolonged possession becomes. Many a nation has had reason to confess the truth of Burkes statement, "Riches, which have neither eyes, nor hands, nor anything truly vital in them, cannot long survive the being of their vivifying powers, their legitimate masters, and their potent protectors." This is equally true of the gathered wealth of hand or brain. Indeed it is not too much to say that experience has shown that an undue attention to knowledge, and undue honour paid to learning, is the characteristic of decline. Whether this be admitted or not, workers are wanted. And the ordinary mind with the ordinary memory cannot accumulate wealth of knowledge, and is but a poor shop; whilst it can be trained to do very good work, and turned out in the world-market a skilled workman at high wages. Few have the time at their command to pile in knowledge. And there is little room for many such accumulators. In fact a great memory is a great maker of common-place, unless overmatched by much original power; and the attempt to load the mind with knowledge often means crowding out all originality and freshness, and putting very little in.

The moment the question is confined to its real issue, the welfare of the many, it becomes simple. Everybody sees that the bulk of mankind never under any circum-
124 Fetiche-worship, stances can be full of learning. But everybody can see that under fair conditions they may reasonably be expected to have their powers well trained, to be active in mind, skilful and capable. This ought to be kept in sight. The

dazzling success of a few, who are revered and honoured through a sort of fetiche-worship, by brains as active, and often far more useful, has served to put the hunt on a false trail. Not the success of a few, deserved or not deserved, fetiche-worship or true honour, is the object of any system, that deals with the human race and their welfare. Extensive knowledge can never be the possession of the many, excellent power of doing skilled work can. If no other arguments were of any value this alone would be conclusive against pumping in knowledge being the first duty of the teacher. Nevertheless the demand for knowledge is the main demand in this generation; and knowledge is producible on demand, when it is there; training is not, or only partially so. This affects teaching, and affects it in a very serious way. All the world knows Socrates. Many schools of philosophy, and a countless number of paths of research, and a countless number of learned men, owe their existence to Socrates. Socrates was a great teacher; but in modern phrase he taught nothing. Socrates is judged to be the greatest teacher the secular world ever had; but he poured no knowledge in, whether by pumping on kettles open or shut. Socrates gave a description of himself as a teacher. He describes himself as a man-midwife for mind; who assisted other people to bring into the world new births of mind. What a noble, yet simple definition of what all teaching should contemplate, new births of mind.

Socrates and examiners. 2 5

He created a science of questioning, which to this hour bears his name; but the answers were theoretically already in the persons questioned. His system presupposed material gathered, but material gathered in order to be made the after-structure of thought. His questions have been searching the world ever since they were put into it, and have quickened the perception of all generations; but Socrates could not have produced a single pupil able to show a modern examiner what he had gained; or to satisfy (satisfy we call it) an examiners demand for knowledge in a modern examination paper. In the first place, Socrates imparted no knowledge at all; and examinations have knowledge as their work and aim. Socrates therefore would be nowhere in an examiners specimen list. Socrates again scornfully rejected everything of the Manual type, and all cut-and-dried rules and formulas, but these are the stock in trade of competitive examinations. Socrates therefore would starve in the enlightened nineteenth century as a teacher; there is no room for teachers. He would have to wear shoes, and–make them, for a livelihood. On the other hand, Socrates the Teacher, not the shoemaker, applied so subtle an instrument of mind by his questions to all he met that he forced them to sift and arrange their ideas. Socrates the teacher sent a plough into the hearts of men, and broke up the ground, and then followed with living breath of strange efficacy, like a spring wind, and called out into new existence all the latent germinating power, all the push of life within. Socrates sent new longings, and new capacities for satisfying longings, into his disciples, not new knowledge in the modern sense: and the receptive 126 Socrates plucked.

mind gathered strength, and clearness, felt its want, and eagerly set about supplying it. So it came to pass that Socrates who taught nothing, produced disciples that learnt everything.

Nevertheless the hard fact remains that Socrates, as a Teacher, would starve in modern England, and be plucked himself in a competitive examination. There would be nothing to produce to–satisfy an examiner. The nature of things makes the extremes of the most perfect training on the one hand, and of producible knowledge on the other, absolutely antagonistic. Or, in other words, the time spent in questioning with a view to train, cannot be spent in carting in knowledge with a view to turn it out again on demand. The importance of the distinction however is not seen in the best men. The best men under either system have made themselves in many ways, irrespective of their system, and would be eminent from their own energy without system, or under any system. What becomes of the average, or the unsuccessful worker, is the real question. The vain attempt to get knowledge results in emptiness, and a stolid unbelief in education. The attempt to get training results in the strength being improved as far as it is capable of being improved, and as much skill being acquired as the case admits of. The first ends in a diseased state of mind; the second in a healthy condition however weak it may be. The inter-penetration of these two rival principles in the great majority of cases renders a subject, which in theory is clear enough, in practice not so clear. There is however little difficulty in seeing which of the two rivals is being pushed to an extreme at any time, if the kind of teaching

The pump rules the world. 127 in vogue is brought into the witness-box; and next, an investigation made as to who are taught, and who are left untaught; and next the tests of the work, and the value set on it, are passed in review briefly.

On the first of these topics there is little room for doubt. The kind of teaching that is more and more coming up over the land is sufficiently indicated by the number of Manuals, which like the frogs in Egypt, come up, and swarm, yea even in the very bedchambers, covering the tables, and littering the floors. These are the natural literature of Class-rooms where the demand for a producible article prevails, and has turned the individual in charge of the class into a kind of clerk of the works, whose main business it is to make the workers tie up little packets of rules, label them neatly, docket them, and pack them into the pigeon-holes of memory, to be brought out whenever asked for, pat! This state of things produces Grammars also bristling with technical terms, labels for everything, endless lists of endless usages, all with their separate names; because a name, whether understood or not, can be produced at call, when the simple principle, by which the thought takes shape in words, would very often explain them all without the need of names, but then this cannot be learnt as a lesson by rote by forty boys at a time; or pulled out as an answer to the question " Give Grammaticuss rule for the Dativus quinquagesimus."

Manuals, and rules, and technical terms; technical terms, rules, and manuals, possess the land and bear potent witness to the theory of the Pump. The next step is a necessary consequence. As soon as individual 128 School failures got rid of.

minds are not the province of a teachers work, nor each separate difficulty his care, as soon as knowledge, rules, and memory engross attention, numbers are immaterial. There is the prescribed packet to be learnt, if a boy does not learn it, it is no business of the clerk of the works, beyond punishing him for not doing it. This soon passes into a neglect of those who cannot, or will not, pigeonhole the daily quota; this naturally advances to finding them very much in the way; the next step is that in the interest of the better boys (so runs the story) they must be got rid of. So the school failures are turned out, and great authority quoted to support the practice; and all the energy of the place is expended on the strong and active, who will distinguish themselves In the knowledge scramble.

The picture is complete when Examinations close the scene. Let it be stated at once clearly, emphatically, without reservation, that examinations are an excellent rough method of deciding whether ignorance is before you. As a pass standard to judge dishonest neglect or culpable idleness, they are efficient. But the moment they are applied as arbiters of merit over a large area, the case is very different; especially if they are taken up as a national system. The space to be covered is wide; vast numbers have to be dealt with. Many different kinds of work, and many different methods of working are brought within their range. Are all the varieties of living growth to be reduced to a lifeless uniformity in order to make them capable of being appraised by Examiners? Even then, where can Examiners be found in sufficient number to do the work, at such a cost as is

Doctors differ. 129 practicable? Moreover there is no agreement at present on the principles by which an Examiner is to examine, or on the points he is to gauge. One University takes an idea of cleverness as its standard. The Examiner is to judge what he considers to be cleverness, and marks by impression. What is cleverness? When that is decided, which it never will be, and the Examiner settles down to his work, by the time he has looked over fifty papers following, his impressions are not infallible, human frailty will have its way sometimes. Another University demands accuracy, and marks by faults, but even the relative value of faults admits of wide difference of opinion. Some Examiners give great credit for showy diction, which others again consider a sign of weakness. Others like logical and concise statements, and so on. In fact the whole domain of examination is a wilderness, with but few landmarks. Again, Examiners are scarce, and the prizes of examinations great. If the same men are constantly employed, as of necessity they must be if the demand for Examiners is very considerable, those whose interest it is to do so get to know their peculiarities, and narrow their work to please them, and to win; and thus throw better teachers out of the race. Again most Examiners are young, and are sent fresh from their books, and their laurels, to pass judgment on what they have not been accustomed to, and tabulate the lifelong labours of men, who having been their equals in intellectual honours twenty, thirty, forty years before, have added since the experience of successful work during those years to their early success in book-work. If books are the work of life, this is not incorrect; but if 130 The patient killed.

teaching mind is the work of life, it is destruction. It is not the purpose of this book to discuss examinations fully, enough has probably been said to show that examinations are very efficient for judging neglect or idleness; are also efficient in a very few well-defined instances in determining a certain kind of merit, but that they break down utterly from many reasons over a wider field. They are also most fascinating exercises of power to those who believe in them. If memory, rules, and neatly packed knowledge make men, up with the flag, enlist our workers under the banner of Examinations.

But if education, and training, are the true aim of mankind, and power in a mans self the prize of life, then no superstition ever ate into a healthy national organism more fatal than the cult of the Examiner. Better in its degree the negro bowing down before the ghastliest fetiche, than the civilized Mumbo-jumboism which thinks it can award over a whole kingdom the palm of mind. Examinations in that case are but another name for death to originality, and all improvement that is original.

CHAPTER X.

THE THEORY OF TEACHING.

The Teacher.

The ground has now been so far cleared as to make it possible to define in some degree what is Teaching, and what is a Teacher. In theory it is both possible and useful to separate Teaching entirely from the acquisition of knowledge. The subject of Teaching is mind, 7 and its work the strengthening of mind, and development T of mental faculties. The mind in this is like the body. And in the case of the body it is possible and useful to separate games and gymnastics entirely from smithy work, or any exercise of strength, which in any particular trade produces a saleable article. And gymnastics, games, pedestrianism, and other forms of bodily exertion, are practised vigorously for the sake of the elastic and varied power given to the body by their practice, totally regardless of the fact that only health and strength, and not 132 Plunder is not skill.

money, result from all the toil. Indeed the one preeminent mark of the highbred man is the simple play of limbs that move with perfect ease, and, as they move, throw off a sense of liberty, and grace, and unconstrained command of strength, able at any moment to do anything that courage may demand of activity, or duty impose on endurance. Whilst some awkwardness of burly power here, or weakness there, betrays the man compelled to gain his livelihood by some particular kind of work to which his muscles must conform their action. Let then the mere acquisition of knowledge be put on one side as not belonging in the first instance to the theory of teaching, any more than wages belong to the theory of training the body. For somewhat the same reason a strong distinction must also be drawn between teaching and learning. There are many ways of learning, where the learner with more or less success occupies himself in working to do this or that branch of bread-winning skill; or in filling in material for use. But all these doings of work no more belong to teaching and mental training of necessity, than filling up a waggon with plunder, and driving it off home, belongs to the artistic skill which by its excellent cunning created the treasures which are plundered and carried off. Teaching means dealing with mind. And Teachers are artificers of mind.

From this point of view the sole question is, how far it is possible to deal with the individual mind. If it is not possible there can be no true teachers. And as long as knowledge is put forward as the object of education, and a given weight required to be weighed out, and taken, teaching is not possible. Some of the school shopkeepers

The block-system. 133 may throw more interest and life into the shop-work than others, but there can be no true teaching. The fact on which all true teaching hinges is this, that every movement which strengthens the mind is a gain; and all true teaching makes movement. Whereas every lump that burdens the mind is a loss; and memory-work is lump-work, and when the mind is blocked by the lumps upset into it, farewell hope of better things. Hearers of lessons are in plenty. But if it is indeed true that the individual mind has to be dealt with, and that no one is a teacher who is prevented from doing this work of moving mind, or who cannot do it, where are the Teachers to come from? Teachers are a very artistic product. They do not grow, like mustard and cress on a bottle, by just sprinkling a few Minutes of Council by authority over the land. A Teacher is a combination of heart, head, artistic training, and favouring circumstances. Like all other high arts life must have free play in the exercise of teaching or teaching cannot be. Mechanic work can be ordered by the foot, and measured, and paid for, by the foot-rule; teaching work cannot. No true Schoolmaster can produce the minds of his Class as specimens on a board, with a pin stuck through them, like a collection of beetles. Shoving in the regulation quantity into the pupils, to be pulled out again on demand, is one thing; clearing the bewildered brain, and strengthening the mind is another.

Teaching means skilful questioning to force the mind to see, to arrange, to act. The Teacher will first take care by some practical home thrusts to waken attention, and compel the boy to consider why he is spending money 134 The Muses were womanly.

and time at school, instead of earning money as a farmers boy in the fields. He will then go on to probe his pupils mind and rouse his curiosity as to school and its work; why Latin and Greek form so large a part of the work, and what is meant by Composition. When this has been questioned out of a boy he is in a condition to begin. True teaching requires liberty, and a delicate hand. Let no rough unfeeling touch knock against the young heart. The Muses surely had womanly sweetness, and gentle hands to endear them to the children of the early world. When the beginner is ready to begin, and these preworking laws have been complied with, then the highest thoughts of the highest men in their truest and most perfect shape have been shown to be the exercise ground of mind; and the love of what is true, and beautiful, and the highest, to be the way by which mind travels through its kingdom to its throne.

First comes reading with its claims. The value of good reading aloud has never been recognised. Good reading is the first training of the beginner, the last crowning excellence and consummate perfection of the finished master of all perfected culture. All skill of heart, of head, of lips, is summed up in the charmed sound of noble utterance falling with thrilling melody on the souls of those over whom a great reader casts his spell. Reading again is the sole giver of words and teacher of word-meaning. When it is considered that words rightly understood mean new thoughts, or new appreciation of thoughts, new subtleties of observation, new powers of collecting treasure, the supreme importance of good reading will be seen. It is computed that the untaught

Language is thought in shape. 135 non-reader uses about 400 words, and has his mind penned within that small enclosure, whilst Shakespear uses 15,000. And every word is a new thought during all the learning stages. And it is certain, that all knowledge which man imparts to man passes through words; and it is certain, that the children of well-to-do families, many of them, are woefully ignorant of the meaning of the commonest words in their own language. The Teacher will read, and will teach his pupils to read. That is the first step. Next the living being comes to be taught how to lead the useful and true life. The Teacher will utilise, expand, vivify, train the life he already has in him. He will rouse the love of thought, inspirit the courage, quicken the energy, feed the curiosity, and call out the endurance of the young traveller on the threshold of a new world. Mind is his subject, thought the work to be done. The moment language is viewed as thought moving, and making its own shape as it moves, the Teacher finds a happy hunting ground full of game; and without book, by simple questions can surprise his pupils into all sorts of discoveries, and make them frame for themselves every rule of Grammar, and arrange their own mind-machinery, at the same time that they can be made to see how every thought that takes shape, the bench they sit on, the picture on the wall, the building they are in, yea, the whole created world, have been obedient each in their way, to the same great laws of composition; and, since all are thoughts taking shape, all have been shaped and wrought on the same principles. And the old worm-eaten stuffed skins of Grammar rules which made words, dead words, their function, and treated 136 Learning to read.

them as dead, apart from living thought, will in time find their way to the curiosity shops, and the garrets.

Interest has to be roused. The Teacher having first made his Class alive to the world-wide sweep of language; and how words, and painting, and sculpture, and all shapes seen by mortal eye are different ways by which thought struggles to make itself felt; and having made clear the wonderful mystery of the commonest talk, and thus opened the mind to unexpected discoveries in common things, will proceed to enlarge the scope of this magic familiarity, and unfamiliar magic. He will take common things, and give them a tongue, or rather will force his hearers to do so. The inkstands which hold their ink, the chairs they sit on, the paper on which they write, the room they are in, the games they play, anything and everything, the commoner the better, can be pressed into service, and by dexterous questioning and crossquestioning be made first of all to give out all the very complex thoughts which they embody by their shape, their material, their history, their making, their present condition, what they have done, have seen, have helped, andc., and secondly, whilst full of exciting novelty, can force with skilful treatment the answerer to overhaul his whole mental stock, disentangle all the confused ideas, sort, separate, arrange, put in order the facts he knows indeed, but has never before known that he knew them, or cast a thought about their having right places, every one of them, and not being a mere loose jumble like potatoes in a sack. In this way the Teacher creates a new world, new in its facts, new in its suggestive power, new in the faculty of order and composition.

The mountain climber. 137

So far of interest in common things. But England has travellers, colonies, great men, great deeds. The Teacher, if allowed, will take them; and having already flung away his grammars until his class has made a grammar for themselves, will proceed to fling away his other rule books, and make the narratives of noble deeds, the lives of great men, vivid travels, descriptive novels, poetry, and all the fascinations of modern discoveries serve as text books, in which the more rigid fact work and bits of necessary clamping are in their proper place. By skilful questions, the Teacher will direct attention, train it, keep it alive, give the observant eye and accurate power, and make all the marvels of sea, and land, mountain, forest, and river, all the fauna and flora of the world, and stars above, and earth beneath, speak through living channels to the lives he is dealing with. New surprises will ever be springing out of the familiar sights and familiar words. Labour there will be; plenty of it; but the labour of the mountain-climber who presses up hill with the delight of an excursion day come at last, and not like a donkey slowly dragged up by strong hands in front, with a whip behind. Teachers, if allowed, will make the toil endurable for the sake of the accompanying freshness, novelty, and strength. But then they must be allowed to teach, allowed to give living realities, allowed to move freely in the world of life, and not shut up in bad Museums with specimens.

Then again in far off lands and ages yet to come, no Teacher will enter his Class-room without being prepared to make his hands help his head, and by rapid sketches to put before his Class in a vivid way all things capable 138 Pictorial reality.

of being illustrated by sight, and pictured to the eye. And Photography will be called in also to imprint the reality of men, and cities, and famous lands on untravel-led readers, until no school shall be thought a school at all which does not use such helps more familiarly than the black boards. In this way the Teacher will by degrees get the minds of his pupils accustomed to the idea of definite impressions and sight. Living in an atmosphere of reality they will follow easily, and with will, those questions by which he draws out of them the pictorial facts of every poem, every narrative they read; instead of staring, as they do now, dumb and stolid, when the picture they cannot draw for themselves, and will not allow to be pulled out of them, is finally painted in words for them, and–not looked at, not appreciated enough to be rejected. Modern Classes will do anything, grovel through any mud, crawl down any ditch, so it be dug for them, rather than stand upright, look round, see the facts and–think; though the moment the right fact is set before the mind, the right answer cannot help but follow; and the lesson how to work has begun. How to work! In those words lies everything. And–no English boy goes to school to learn how to work. They go to learn lessons and have lessons heard, and corrected. But the Teacher teaches how to work. Let it not be supposed that all the wide space in word-land which no picture can reach has been forgotten. No. But life reaches it, it is dry bones no more. At the touch of life all the dead rules and musty catalogues of dead names vanish away, and a new spirit passes into the remainder full of intelligent interest. The subtle play of words as they dance

Dragged or guided. 139 out of one language into another, the exquisite sameness which is not the same draws by a resistless charm those who once see it. And the pictorial mind trained to draw pictures can live a very real life with thoughts that breathe and burn; or at least can feel the sinewy growth of greater power of life conferred by such companionship. The difference is unspeakable between working blindfold, working in chains, and being guided through a glorious country, though the road is the same, and the landscape is the same. And it is the difference between doing lessons and having a Teacher. The Teacher, if allowed to do so, will lead on his workers by intelligent exercise to a willing acceptance at last of the toil which alone makes strong. And they standing on the verge of the great unknown land of life, and thought, and song, and hero deeds, for the sake of that which they have already seen will be ready to go on and do the self-denying work, and bear. with hardihood the necessary labour of exploring the territory they have to make their own by exploring; and will not count it self-denial, or hardihood, for the joy they take in the active energy of the doing it. And so passing from happy life to happy life through labour, and ever increasing demands on strength and courage, the workers are led on by a true teacher to play their part like men, when their hour comes, and be they strong, or be they weak, to bring trained powers and do good service, each in their place.

This is the Theory of Teaching.

And a Teacher is one, who has liberty, and time, and heart enough, and head enough, to be a master in the kingdom of life; one, whose delight it has been to study 140 Dreams not illegal.

mind, not in books, but in the strange realities of dull and ignorant pupils; one, who has found joy in darting a ray of light into dark corners, and wakening up hope and interest in the scared lesson-learners who have not learnt; one, who can draw out latent, power from the lowest, and quicken, inspirit, and impart, new senses to the highest.

A Teacher has as his subject life and mind.

A Teachers life is in living beings, not in printers ink.

A Teacher is an Artificer of mind and noble life.

Above all, a Teacher never lets a single life of those put into his hands be spoiled, or wasted, or flung aside through neglect, or scorn.

A Teacher is the helper and friend of the weak.

That is a Teacher.

There is no law against dreaming. Though law and public opinion make Teaching impossible, though there be no Teacher and can be no Teacher any more, dreams are beyond law. Men still can dream.

PART II.

CHAPTER I.

THE PRACTICE OF TEACHING.

The Workman, and the Reader.

The general theory of practical education has been roughly stated, and an outline sketched of the main facts which decide absolutely what a nation ought to have in view for the training of its leading classes. The fallacy of the maxim that knowledge is power, in the ordinary acceptation of that maxim, has been shown, and the need of drawing out the power that is in the man himself, exercising it, and implanting new faculties, (for they amount to nothing less,) has been pointed out. It is perfectly possible to lay down laws for producing bodily strength. It must be no less possible to find out the conditions which are required to produce mental strength, as soon as that is seen to be the object. When these are established with certainty, as without doubt they can be, many difficulties which at present appear insuperable, will vanish. No attempt however has been made to 144 Life touches life.

deal with the existing state of things, or to argue out the question by exhaustive reasonings. Neither is the construction of a perfect school any part of the plan. Whether what has been laid down is practicable, or not, at the present time, or what is going to be stated is practicable, or not, at the present time, does not fall within the compass of this work. There is no intention to win adherents. This treatise is a workers treatise addressed in the first instance to workers; and it will be interpreted according to their work. If they are in harmony with it it will be felt by them, like the sunshine and the air, as part of their health and their strength, needing no arguments beyond their own feelings and experience. It will glide out of one life into another with the silent conviction of life. Or if they differ, they will nevertheless understand, and think over the matter, and readjust perhaps the focus of their thoughts. At all events, being workers, being in earnest, they will not proceed to dress up straw men, call them their opponents case, and demolish them, after the fashion of those amateurs, whom omniscient ignorance sets in the judges seat. Those again who are honourably engaged in a routine not their own, and are doing honourable work under defective systems, unconscious often that they are defective, will respect a workers words. Some few there are, good men also, who crystallized by habit, and circumstances stronger than their own power to deal with, have already made up their minds, and are committed to another line, by all they have ever said or done, by all their hopes, and all their fame; they unconsciously, like the wolf in the fable, do not want arguments but dinner. Well let them dine: the victim

The material and the work. 145 has still one hope left that he may prove somewhat indigestible.

This treatise is above all things addressed to workers first; and a workers words to workers have an existence of their own. The fustian coat is out of place in the drawing room, but feels at home amongst the machinery and the oil. And everything pertaining to work, sooner or later, comes to a question of the material to be worked, and the means at disposal for doing the work, the machinery and oil. The first question of the practice of teaching is, what kind of material comes into the teachers hands, combined with its counterpart, what kind of work is practical teaching.

The kind of material that has to be dealt with provides the first test of experience and inexperience, observant work and hack work, practice and dreams. The skilled workman is always known by his judgment on his material. What is a carpenter who cannot judge wood? a builder who cannot judge bricks and mortar? a teacher who cannot judge mind? For minds have to be dealt with, if minds have to be trained; and all else, books, or men, must be adapted to the work of training minds, as minds really are, not as brain-spinners imagine them to be. The blind cannot be taught to draw, however skilful the artist that teaches; music is no good to the deaf. And in like manner it is quite possible that the authorities, who have the popular ear, have mistaken the task before them. They may play with exceeding skill, and yet, perchance because of their very skill, be quite out of reach of the poor deaf boy-world below them, and tootle up above to the great delight of all–but those 146 Tootling to the deaf.

that need it most; who persist in refusing to hear the voice of the charmer charm he never so wisely; perhaps for the somewhat conclusive reason that they cannot hear. The first question is what the minds to be dealt with are; not what they ought to be; but what they are; the actual material that generations of neglect, or idleness, or wrong methods, or dull homes, or money-loving cities, or any other form of stunted life may send forth as the average type of boy pupil. A wide space lies between dreamland and factland here. It would be much pleasanter to blow the after-dinner trumpet of " glory to the present, the past to the dogs," than to make feeble efforts to wake the world, and be bitten perchance without waking it; but it is impossible to do so. The whole question of right or wrong turns on the kind of material that comes to be manufactured, and whether the manufacturer can, and does, do the work without waste, honestly, and in all cases. The raw material itself is a very artificial product to begin with, and represents faithfully in its fineness or coarseness a long past history. Human minds are not hap-hazard waifs; the infant just born is the heir of congenital conditions of good or evil; and whether those conditions are to be passed on better, or worse, is a very vital question. An example may make this clearer, and illustrate how complex the problem is, even at the very beginning, how great the divergence can be, and what momentous issues depend on meeting the facts fairly, neither shutting the eyes to the truth, nor getting rid of it, or seeming to get rid of it, by hustling it out of sight. Take the case of Mozart as representing typically the perfection of child-

Mozart and the tom-tom player. 147 life, the best raw material that can come into a trainers hand. It is possible to imagine exceptional musical ability coming into existence in any nation beneath the sky. Even the most savage tribe might have, and very likely does have, its gifted genius, its greatest master of sound, born to it. But what is he? He merely represents a new phase of tom-toms, an advance on the rude melodies of his fathers. But a Mozart, who at five; and seven years of age, can play, and compose the noble and refined harmonies of modern music, has born within him the living spirit of generations of genius and skill, and begins life with natural powers of a different order from those of the musical savage. Mozart, and the tom-tom player, practically represent the extremes of good and bad material between which the work of the practical worker lies. As this is the case it is easy to see how useless it would be to come forward, and elaborate a scheme of education out of the inner consciousness in the blissful hallucination that nothing had to be considered but what books should be used by classes consisting of intelligent Mozarts.

Brain-spinners, who have never taught a child, might just as well go to bed and dream, and publish their dreams, as prescribe what should be taught, and how, in total ignorance of the problems to be solved in teaching a child.

St Augustine hit the point, when he said of teaching, "a golden key which does not fit the lock is useless, a wooden key, which does, is everything." He might have added with advantage, that using one big key for all locks is idiotic. The key that fits the lock, whatever 148 Glitter warned off.

may be the popular idea, or the action of Government, or the talk of philosophers, is the question of the day. Those who care for this will not despise the wooden key, because it is wooden. The true teacher has to fit himself to the mind he is teaching, not the pupil to fit himself to the teacher, when the question is taken from the teachers point of view. The kind of lock and the wooden key that fits come first, according to St Augustine.

These pages however commonplace, or unlovely, are, as far as they are anything, locksmiths work. Those who want gold and glitter must go elsewhere. They are addressed to practical workers. For the rest, if any like them not, let Aristotle answer

Tandv H n65ov,

jit jrwapiotos as ouris irdvta voija-j, 5" aj niinavos 6s eu tlirom

8s 6V Ke /Aijr aiiris 1 0 77 firir CixXou

iv 6v/Uf j3d Xi; Tai o 6 aur

CHAPTER II.

THE PRACTICE OF TEACHING.

The Raw Material, Structure, Teaching.

The question of the teachers work at any given moment depends entirely on those he has to teach. And the capacity of those he has to teach depends, as has been shown, on the work of preceding generations, and the temper of the times in which the teacher lives. It is useless to speculate beforehand. Minds are not like books, which remain the same, and once known, are always known. They are what they are, not what they are imagined to be; and every mind is somewhat different. Apparently, the theory that individual minds have to be treated individually, and the mental powers in every case developed, has not found favour. No traces at all events of such care can be discovered. Examples of splendid intellectual power are not wanting. There is abundant evidence of the full mind, and of refined learning, and habits of work imparted to a chosen few. But no sign r 50 Inherited failure.

of the trained mind giving to every one a sense of educated power can be seen. The prevailing feeling of the majority undoubtedly is not a feeling of elasticity and success: and the majority determine infallibly the atmosphere in which men live, and the temper in which the daily life moves, and meets the days demands. Generations which get nothing, though much is gone through, are not only ignorant; that is a fault easily remedied, but every successive generation of much enduring failures, or partial failures, passes on a more confirmed unreadiness to take the trouble of trying to learn. Not ignorance, but un-teachableness, is the evil transmitted by bad or imperfect measures; not a mere vacuum of no music, but a tomtom nature, is the inheritance of perpetual tom-toms. A most amusing, a most melancholy chapter might be written to prove the tom-tom condition in which the bulk of the material first comes to hand, the utter absence of any foundation of real interest, or belief, combined with complete vegetating power of contented acquiescence in thinking and doing nothing. So they begin; then a large proportion goes on, passing a squatters life, mere vagabonds, and strangers, in whatever part of the great wilderness of knowledge their tattered tent may be at the moment pitched. The parish authorities are always at them, and always in vain, they end as they began with no home in the land, no settled hold of anything belonging to learning, no love for the pastures up and down which they have been hunted without knowing why and wherefore. Examples without number might be adduced to support and justify the statement that there is no feeling for education, no aptitude for it, no belief that

Tlie cantering whale. 151 anything worth having can be got, in the boy-material that mostly comes under notice. No doubt there is a heavy tradition that, like terrier puppies in old days, it is the thing for every boy to undergo the process of having his ears cropped, to say nothing of another. appendage; but this fashionable docking is entirely different from any conception of real increase in life power, and the eager, keen, hunter spirit of Platos Athenian boys. Only two instances however shall be cited, as typical of this state of things, and samples of drawers full, lest the absurdity of the examples should cause the sad truth they bear witness to to be lost sight of, and a chorus of laughter titillate the parental world, instead of sorrowful misgivings, thoughtful attention, and a sitting in sackcloth and ashes, striving for better things. The first example is as follows. A class of from 23 or 24 boys in number, whose ages averaged 15 years, or thereabouts, were engaged on a passage in Ovid. The boy construing said something about a dolphin, which raised suspicion in the masters mind; who thereupon in a quiet voice asked him demurely, How many legs a dolphin had? "Two," was the immediate answer. A gentle smile beneath the skin of his face, in spite of the questioners self-command, began involuntarily to twinkle through; upon which the boy promptly corrected his answer to "Four." These novelties of natural history roused a thirst for further knowledge, especially as no one seemed the least surprised. A few more questions revealed, that only one boy in the class knew what a whale was. Many did not know whether it was a sea, or a land, animal. One intrepid explorer boldly 152 The carnivorous stag.

stated it was a quadruped; and, what was more, was master of the fact that the word " quadruped " meant an animal with four legs. This is no extraordinary example. It has merely been selected as more likely to come home to the general reader than hundreds at hand. There is a grand imaginativeness in the mental picture of a whale cantering gaily ale ng in boy-wonder-land. So also of the next. A boy of 16 construed a passage, in which a wild boar and a stag were mentioned, into most undiluted nonsense. The master dropped all research into the hopeless morass of the Latin, and grappled with what, for want of a better name, must be called the boys mind, with the following result. The questioning was quite friendly, and carried on without any accompanying fear of penalties. The boy philosopher did not know whether the stag chased the wild boar, or the wild boar the stag, or the chances of one hunting the other. He did not know whether the stag eat the wild boar, or the wild boar the stag. He had not the remotest idea, he said, what a wild boar was. But he brightened up on the stag, and said, he knew it was an animal with horns. On being further asked, what he would give a tame stag to eat, if he had one, he answered doubtfully, " grass, he thought." But on flesh being mildly suggested, said at once, " he was not sure that he would not give him flesh."

The ordinary English boy from well-to-do homes does not understand much of the language used in ordinary conversation even. But all knowledge comes through words. How can unknown words impart knowledge? The unknown cannot teach the unknown. To attempt it is to set up a manufactory of stupidity. But the schools

Beau JBrummels cravats. 153 are only partially to blame for this ignorance. Out of what homes have the carnivorous stags, and four-footed whales, and English who cannot talk English come? If the boys who come to school cannot talk English, and the schools start by assuming they can; and the schools are rigidly tied down by public opinion, and law, to a fixed line of work to be got through in a match against time, the schools cannot deal with this question, or teach. They are prevented by law, examinations, and public opinion. Time is lord of all things, especially in schools. What does time demand? If indeed not lessons but mens lives are the material dealt with, and each life is of priceless value, and twenty must not be spoiled, like Beau Brummels cravats, in making one perfection of a neat tie, then the question of time does press like a mountain on schools; and spoiled lives must continue to be the product of the attempt to make education consist in the unknown thrusting in the unknown into unwilling receptacles. Yet ignorance is the least part of the evil. Not ignorance, however great, is the difficulty to be faced; but the nature, the dull, contented nature, which is satisfied with dulness, which neither wants to know, nor is ashamed of not knowing; the heavy, moveless clay, which is quite unresisting, yet hopelessly sticky

But the fathers of these boys have been at school. What were the schools, which have succeeded in filling England with these Mozarts of literature? That they have not done their work is clear. Who is in fault? Can the work be done? Is it possible under present conditions to pay attention to the mind of each boy? Are the schools in fault? or the powers 154 Captains are not ships.

which control the schools? Public opinion? Market price? Government? Legislation? There have been something like thirty years of legislation. Has legislation cleared or obscured the question? What great principles of school construction have been laid down? Does any one know the cost of teaching any subject well to each boy, and not neglecting any one of the many? Has the subject of teaching each boy, the possibility of doing so, the means necessary, and the cost of the means, come into the horizon of discussion? nay the horizon of speculation even? What is the unit, by which cost must be calculated? After thirty years of legislation these simple postulates of work, this alphabet of education, are doubtless mere household furniture in every home, common property, mottoes on the wall, scrolled over the doors. Or is any structure necessary in a school? Does it not take shape as a natural growth? Yet a natural growth has a seed to start from. What is the school seed? These are very serious questions, and many more might be asked. Grand words from hero-worshipped Headmasters no more answer them, than a Captains seamanship turns an old tub of a sailing vessel into a firstrate ironclad. Talking of truth, and honour, and trust, is one thing, and having the structure true, and honourable, and trust-deserving, another. The Captain is not the ship. The make of the ship, not the Captain, determines the kind of manoeuvres it can do, and what can be done in it. And the make of a school determines in like manner what can be taught, and what training can be given. No glorification of canonized Head-masters touches the question of carnivorous stags. Solomon

First, second, and last. 155 himself could not teach four walls, or the boys inside them, if wanting individual attention, individual attention cannot be given on account of numbers. Each mind is different. The degrees of capacity are different. The degrees of apathy are different. The causes of the apathy (are different. Platos young Athenians are not English schoolboys. Nor, it may be retorted, are English schoolmasters Platos. Be it so. That is just the point which requires to be driven home. How can English schoolmasters be turned into Platos, in method, at all events? Real teaching is wanted. What then is real teaching? And how can the carnivorous stags be exterminated? If teaching means calling out dormant faculties, and strengthening mind, it is obvious that pumping indiscriminately on a class, though the veritable waters of Helicon be pumped, is not teaching. Mind is the teachers subject. He must be able to deal with mind. The first thought of the teacher must be those he has to teach. The second thought must be those he has to teach. The last thought must be those he has to teach. What he teaches is not his subject a bit more than the medicine a doctor gives is the doctors patient. A teachers first maxim is, "If the boys dont learn it is my fault;" his comforting axiom, "The worse the material the greater the skill of the worker." He addresses himself in every possible way to get at the inner life. He tries to find a chink here, to scrape open a little rift there, for a ray of light to get in. By praise and blame, and skilful application of wits in unexpected ways, he endeavours to meet the boy on his own ground, beat him there where his own ideas are encamped, enlist him, and lead him on to conquest.

156 Pupils not books.

The whole secret of teaching lies in one sentence, find in the pupils mind a irov Otcu, and everything becomes possible. It will be observed that from this point of view the pupil and the teacher are everything, and that their relations to each other decide the whole question. The books and the knowledge are nowhere till this fact is established What matters it that the teacher is dispensing nectar, if the pupil is chasing carnivorous stags? The problem of the present day is a simple one, simply stated, without any circumlocution. It is this, how to reach the mind of each boy.

CHAPTER III.

THE PRACTICE OF TEACHING.

The Lecturer.

The teachers subject, as has been shown, is not books, but mind. On the other hand the lecturers subject in the first instance is not mind, but books. This distinction is vital, and the most important results follow. Broad is the dyke, and deep, that cuts across between the teacher and the lecturer, dividing them by a bridgeless space. They stand on the same level; at a little distance they appear in the same field; to the ordinary eye they are engaged in the same work, with the same surroundings, and the same objeet. But they are divided for ever in theory, and in practice It has already been shown that the subject of the teacher is the mind of the individual; that his first, second, and last thought must be mind, and how to get at mind. But the first, second, and last thought of the 158 The ready-made-clothes shop.

lecturer is how to get out his book-work in the clearest and most presentable form. His books, and the way he handles his books must be his subject. This arises from the nature of things. The lecturer has to deal with knowledge. He is a knowledge-master and must conform himself to the conditions of knowledge. Knowledge demands that the work to be done should be put out from beginning to end without flaw, and with perfect skill. To do this implies that the worker uninterrupted by any external consideration should do the work himself, shape it, polish it, and with great artistic skill turn out a work of art. He addresses a mass. The component parts of his audience, the single minds with their difficulties, are nothing to him. He assumes, and is justified in assuming, if his lectures are voluntary, that the audience are prepared to understand him by previous acquirements. The general character of his instruction must indeed be adapted to his audience. But for this it is enough for him to know their general character. Nothing more is required. He is like a ready-made-clothes shop. If he wishes to succeed, richness of-material, and a graceful hitting off the average taste must make up for want of individual fit. His knowledge must be cut into the most acceptable pattern. This requires much command of the book to be communicated, much tact in the fashioning, and a taking and effective style of delivery. But when done it is done. The book, and the knowledge, and the skilful narrative are the sole business of thc lecture. The audience must take care of themselves. A good lecturer puts out his work wonderfully well, and those who profit by it come

Lecturing a performance. 159 already prepared, and adapt themselves to what they hear. Is this last line a definition of the English schoolboy? or of any schoolboy?

But it is in this that the difference lies between teacher and lecturer, between taught and belectured. The teacher makes the taught do the work, and occupies himself in showing them how to do it, and taking care that they do do it. His work is to direct, suggest, question, inspirit-and he adapts himself in every possible way to the individual minds, never resting till he has made them master of the skill required, and seen them become capable of working on their own account. The lecturer leaves his audience, and they leave him; and he goes his way entirely regardless of their fate, only concerned with having performed with credit to himself. The distinction is vital. Excellence in the one is a complete reversal of excellence in the other. The lecture is clear cut, logical, precise, beautifully connected, yet avoiding all close and laborious exactness. Teaching takes any shape whatever, is fragmentary, changing as the difficulties of the pupils minds change, and disregards all precise plan, provided that a close, laborious, and exact exercise of mind is the result. The lecturer does the work, and goes. The teacher makes the pupils work, and stands or falls by what they do.

A most important practical result at once is developed from these facts. The number that can be dealt with at one sitting is fixed. A teacher can only teach in one hour as many as he can make take part personally in the work, and question, and look to individually in one hour.

160 The audience, the class.

A lecturer can take with advantage any number within pleasant reach of his voice. In fact numbers are an advantage to the lecturer. They inspirit him. A lecturer lecturing to one is an absurdity. But a teacher1 teaching one may be perfection. A large audience excites ambition in the lecturer, and gives an artificial glow to the familiar theme. But a large class overwhelms the teacher with despair.

If this is put in a concrete form the effect will be manifest at once, and the serious nature of the distinction appear. A lecturer can lecture to one hundred, two hundred, any reasonable number of hundreds, in one hour. They all hear him, and that is all they have to do. A teacher can teach twenty-five at the outside in the same time. This decides the question of cost. If one hundred is taken as a low estimate of a possible audience, and twenty-five as the maximum of a class, then the cost to each hearer of a lecturer is one quarter the cost of a teacher, if both are paid on the same scale per head. And a boy in a class must pay four times as much for his lesson, as a hearer in a lecture-room. It is no wonder that poor teaching gets jostled out of the market. Yet if parents took to heart the real manner in which the question of cost acts, they would think long and well before they gave their verdict. The belectured boy, unless prepared, and interested, goes away empty, having got nothing. Amongst the average throng of unprepared young minds that are annually sent to swell the muster-roll of large classes, if ten per cent. really gain much, and twenty per cent. gain something, a balance of seventy per cent. remains who have gained nothing.

Diners and dinner less. 161

This seventy per cent, accordingly, who retire from the table, dinnerless, have paid for the intellectual dinner of the rest. So as a hundred pay, and thirty dine, the charge per head can be low. Later on the empty ones are returned on hand fit for comparatively little, even if they have not been summarily ejected from the school, after the fashion of modern legislation. This money question underlying the whole question of teaching versus pumping is very serious. For nothing which is not worked on true principles of trade will last. Martyrs, who will work for nothing, cannot be reckoned on as part of the negotiable commodities in the market; and moreover a system worked by martyrs in the first generation generally ends, as has been mentioned before, by being worked by cheats in the second. One thing is certain, the teacher and the lecturer represent two opposite poles; there is an antagonism in principle between a subject put forth attractively, where the master does the work and the disciple listens, and the problem of a dull mind solved, and dormant faculties roused to efficient powers, where the disciple does the work, and the disciples mind is the subject, and the teacher is a practitioner on mind. Two different kinds of character are called into play. The teacher must be full of human sympathy, inwardly exhaustless in kindness and patience, willing to bear anything but refusal to be taught, and fertile in resources even for that. The lecturer must be full of book sympathy, and intensely alive to the writings he deals with; but he may be intolerant to the last degree of slow humanity and blundering helplessness; it is no part of his business to succour the weak. Un- 162 Flinging peas.

happily whenever the start is made from the book sympathy and the hoards of knowledge, teaching, in its true sense, is exterminated. The moment numbers shut off attention to individual minds, it is obvious that the mind problem is not attended to. This means in school classes, that rules, rules, rules, and the fixed tale of bricks must be the staple of the work; and whoever cannot, or will not, comply, and take in and put out on demand the legal quantity, must go; and ought to go, for to stay with no power of getting the rule work done is wasted time. Nevertheless this means, when translated into plain English, that, whereas a teachers work is to train the dull minds, even more than the quick ones, which train themselves, this work of training the dull is not done, and not attempted to be done, and the failures, which were failures because the work was not done, are got rid of; just as an amateur carpenter beginning flings aside the wood he has spoiled. The low class is the teachers pride, and the pumpers dismay. The nauseous demand for higher work, so often reiterated, betrays the poor deluded honour-man whose one idea is knowledge; and who walks into the school, like an old farmers wife into her poultry-yard with her apron full of peas, to be flung out indiscriminately, with a cheerful consciousness of beneficent superiority, and picked up, or–not–as may happen.

The dull, or closed mind is a very curious exercise of skill on the part of the teacher; but a neglected nuisance on the part of the lecturer. Which is it to be? teaching? or lecturing? boys? or books? see ye to it fathers and mothers. It concerns you. What becomes of the birds

Birds that wont feed. 163 who will not be fed? or who cannot pick up knowledge like peas?

No boy ought to leave school untrained. Mind is the teachers subject, and the teacher ought to be able to deal with mind. Which is it to be? the teacher? or the lecturer?

CHAPTER IV.

THE PRACTICE OF TEACHING.

Thought-stamps; not Argument.

The teacher preparing for his work has passed by; now let his class stand up and give some account of themselves. There are four main facts brought out by experience in dealing with the young mind.

First, the reasoning power of the young, the power, that is, to follow a logical chain of reasoning, is nonexistent.

Secondly, the young have no power of attention. Attention has to be learnt as much as any other lesson.

Thirdly, the memory of the young is very good, if they care for what they are doing.

Fourthly, there is no power in a young boy to master a subject thoroughly.

Thoroughness requires a strength which does not exist. These four facts, for facts they are, are the four first problems to be dealt with by the teacher.

Pictorial knowledge. 165

The complete absence, practically, of the reasoning faculty, so far as learning by means of it goes, determines at once the whole character of good teaching at the beginning. There must be simple statements, and simple explanations. The early stages require the new ideas and facts to be put like little pictures before the pupil, without any attempt to show the mechanism, as it were, by which the effect is produced. Logical progression is out of the horizon. The all-important factor of the mind to be taught must be the starting point. If processes are shown, it must also be, so to say, pictorially, in some subject already very familiar. The inside of common things is intensely interesting to the curious child, witness the number of toys that have been the victims of scientific research, and broken, to find out what was inside. But then they were toys, thorough property, entirely in the power, manual and mental, of the owners. Wherever there is the feeling of thorough property, there is also the wish for thorough knowledge, and the child delights in having the structure of the familiar thing laid bare. But even then, much as they like to know all about what is their own, the knowledge is a knowledge by sight, not a matter of reasoning. This then is the principle of all early work, either eye-sight, or mental sight. Either actually show the bit of teaching, which often can be done; or let the bit be a little plain statement, a kind of stamp, which the mind can see without trouble. Trouble enough will come in due time. This principle requires the teacher to lay aside the fascinating shapeliness of a clear-cut system, and submit himself to the yoke of the boy-mind. Rigid, formulated, square statements, cannot 166 A dull boy s mind a wise mans problem.

find their way with their corners into the little tortuous windings of the little mind, with all its blind mazes, passages that lead to nothing, obstructions of previous ideas, mobs of small idolatries, idolatries of play, idolatries of day-dreams, combined with absolute incapacity to bear the unyielding thrust of logic in its fine tissues. The teacher must indeed have a logical plan of his own, which he does not lose sight of; but the actual teaching has to be imparted bit by bit, as the learner is fitted to take it, with many illustrations, and digressions, which are not digressions, but roundabout ways of arriving at points, where the direct path is blocked. A dull boys mind is a wise mans problem. Mind is the teachers real subject; and how to excite thought, and arouse interest, without making much demand on the logical faculty, the first aspect which the work of mind presents. Perhaps, considering what is almost universally done, the first rule to be laid down is a prohibition. Never try to fill the little mind with lumber, under colour of its being of use by and by. Lumber does not excite thought, lumber does not interest, lumber does breed disgust; nothing should be put into the mind which is not wanted immediately, and which is not also the easiest way of meeting the want. The pupil ought to be made to feel that thought is a pleasure, and a power; and that learning means being taught to think by easy steps. For example. He knows that the having learnt to read and write has opened up to him treasures, which he would not now give up, and therefore he can be made to believe that the new tasks, however distasteful, are going to do the same thing in a still higher degree, and land him in

Thought not distasteful. 167 unknown empires. But why should they be so distasteful? Thought in its true sense is not distasteful. When mind enters into the works of mind, and receives life from them, the new life is not distasteful. The whole mighty realm of imagination is thought, whether it be the imagination, which creates the Midsummer Nights Dream, or the imagination, which sets the baby child in the nursery on the floor, and surrounds it with a living kingdom in the guise of broken toys, and makes it lisp to a much-battered doll, "You are the Queen." Imagination is not distasteful. There are plenty of thought-pictures in common things for any one who knows how to paint them, or, better still, make his pupils paint them. And thought is the beginning, thought the middle, and thought the end of a learners work. Let not the teacher pile in lumber that is not thought. The learner can be made to see without difficulty that new thoughts, and the power of receiving thoughts and thinking thoughts, are a gain and a pleasure in the long run, because he has already found them to be a pleasure, or ought to have done so. The next step is easy. The learner can be made to understand the obvious truth, that language, and literature are the great exercise ground of thought, and mind; inasmuch as all thought passes through language. Words are the every-day and all-day messengers of common life, as well as the varied and intelligent expression afterwards of the thoughts of the greatest thinkers. There is no reason in the nature of things why the child in the nursery should not understand, aye, and feel gratefully the meaning of Teaching; and be taught through the familiar sights and words the pleasure of being taught, and led on 168 Do-nothing labour.

to work with interest in collecting new material, and in thinking over what has been collected. This truth is not impaired by the fact that much has to be taken on trust at first, much to be learnt on faith, which cannot be fully explained at the time. It only means that there are grounds for this faith; that these grounds should be made plain; and that as the demands for labour and patience increase, the faith should increase in proportion, from the sense experienced daily of an increase in power and pleasure, which a skilful teacher will unobtrusively keep up. There is no more reason in the nature of things why a boy should rejoice in the weak and inactive mind, than in the weak and inactive body. If bodily training consisted in carrying heavy stones from one hole to another, and, as fast as they were thrown in, pulling them out, and taking them back again, there would be no lack of feeble bodies. Every boy would be as weak as a resolute evasion of being employed in doing nothing laboriously could make him. How much of child labour in knowledge, falsely so called, is a doing nothing laboriously, with much solemn jargon, and much real infliction. The simple formula, " give a beginner something to think about," sets this all straight at once. Something to think about! This cannot be a sawn-out board of dry knowledge. Something to think about! This must be an object of interest, partly understood therefore, partly new, familiar, but unknown. Nature has given this in the learners native language, and its treasures of beautiful thought. Whenever the nations believe in the training of mind being the first thing, and the heaping up of knowledge the second, the language and literature of

Nature first, museums afterwards. 69 each nation will be studied first. The mediaeval process of self-flagellation will be left off, and work made aseasy and delightful as possible, with the absolute certainty that when the preliminaries are over, the stubborn realities of the greater achievements of mind and their demands will give plenty of labour, and plenty of pain, if pain is wanted. The beginner ought to be made to feel that the gain is worth any pain by the time he is called on to make the sacrifice. This principle excludes all cut-and-dried definitions, packets of rules, and formulated results. It requires, if such an illustration may be allowed, that the young should learn natural history and botany in the woods and fields first, and not be set down in a Museum to dried specimens, and stuffed animals, and elaborate classification, till they have learnt the value of a Museum, and its meaning.

There is another subject almost as much within reach as language, which is entirely neglected as a training subject for mind, though equally open to all, which demands nicety of hand and eye, great mechanical skill, and introduces the dullest at once to strange discoveries in common things, that greatest point of true Education. It is marvellous that the grand training of Drawing has never taken its place as a teaching power. The learner is met on the very threshold by the truth of truths, that he has eyes that see not, and hands which cannot do his will He finds out that the lines go in a way he knows not, though they are known. He looks at a wall, and sees what he sees, but is utterly unable to record what he sees; all is wrong the moment he begins. The very chair he sits in is a puzzle of untold difficulty. He is 170 Drawing a great teaching power.

brought face to face with that grand fact of the wondrous perfection of accurate power in the midst of which he has moved unknowingly, and he comes in sight of the highest truth that man can attain to, a perception of his own unconscious ignorance, utter incapacity, and clumsiness. A fresh secret leaps out of every leaf, there is not a pebble which is not turned into a world. The transformation which follows immediately the smallest child is made to Draw, and set to observe the what? and the why? in things, and attention turned on to the endless discoveries of ignorance which are disclosed in this way, is more rapid, and complete perhaps than in any other exercise of mind. This is, or may be, the beginning. Later on the art of composition, that is, of intelligent arrangement of thought, is more effectually illustrated by a picture, than in any other way. It is no concern of this treatise to glorify the painters skill; but the neglected world of truest teaching, which is waiting to be used whenever Drawing is taught as a matter of mind, not of hand, and is recognized as one of the first great exercise grounds of mind, does belong to the Teachers province. The impossibility of jumbling ideas together in a Drawing without detection in the first place, and a detection, which can be made plain to the eye, in the second, is a virtue, which would be very valuable in much teaching work in language; and most important of all, the one vivid impression with everything leading up to it and back from it, which is the life of a picture, is the life of a lesson also. But how often a lesson has nothing pictorial, firm, or unblurred in it. Many men pass their days without ever having composed a lesson in

The lesson and the picture. 171 their lives. Their statements are all equally forcible, or equally feeble, as the case may be. Faults are knocked about at random, as they occur, without the slightest attempt to mark some strongly, and to drop others into the background. All is on the same level. No definite piece of teaching brought out, no high light; no definite style of blunder unobtrusively stamped out. But in Drawing the difference between a true composition and this chinese-plate work is seen"at once; and the necessity for decision and skill in arrangement self-evident. Every good Drawing is a model lesson, in which what has to be taught is imprinted at once by a single skilful stroke. And no one knows the skill which has blended so many parts into one thought-stamp, until the confusion of untrained work is seen. There is no work so untrained as the attempt of a master to uncoil a chain of reasoning, and put it into the boy mind. Long before the end is reached the beginning has disappeared. Nothing that is not valuable piecemeal is valuable in teaching the young. The best teaching will be like St Pauls Epistles, where every single verse is powerful and plain, however subtle or elaborate the argument of the whole may be. Good teaching will at least have each impress powerful and plain, and be working secretly towards a given end.

A feeble stroke is useless. Too much giving of reasons is worse than useless. A Teacher must be content to omit much, and not be concerned about the glossiness of his work. The mind of a working, vigorous little boy is much like his clothes, very untidy, but very serviceable, entirely regardless of every thing but the object at 172 Composing lessons.

the moment. No doubt order and tidiness are part of the training; but dress boots wont do for turnip fields, or mountains. Strength is needed first. Strong ideas are wanted, put forth by an unseen plan. Every good teacher will compose his lessons, and compose them on this principle. Interest must be excited, faith inspired, mind dealt with.

CHAPTER V.

THE PRACTICE OF TEACHING.

Inattention, Indifference, Sleep.

The next fact that has to be dealt with is attention. Much misapprehension exists on this head. Because people are attentive, when strong interest is roused, there is a common idea that attention is natural, and inattention a culpable fault.

But the boy mind is much like a frolicking puppy, always in motion, restless, but never in the same position two minutes together, when really awake. Naturally his body partakes of this unsettled character. Attention is a lesson to be learned; and quite as much a matter of training as any other lesson. A teacher will be saved much useless friction if he acknowledges this fact, and instead of expecting attention, which he will not get, starts at once with the intention of teaching it; being well assured that it would be just as sensible to look for the Latin Grammar to be spun off the reel by the 174 Leaky dykes.

light of nature, without book, as for attention to be got without training. A teacher will treat this as a lesson, and exercise all his skill in teaching it, and be patient with beginners, and command it by life, good humour, and go.

It is curious how entirely in most cases the progress of the lesson reflects the temper of the master. If this is true, it is obvious that the personal power of the master in all bits of small discipline and the general swing of the class, will decide absolutely in a fair time the habits of the class. A sleepy manner, however strong the real interest taken by the master may be, produces in the taught either laziness and apathy in the lazy, or tricks in the puppy section. It is most disastrous in anything belonging to discipline to overlook beginnings. No leak ever broke up a dyke more certainly than trifles passed over break up the order of a class. There is however a worse fault still, a fault which is almost universal; this is, to legalise insubordination by having a set of small routine punishments, and imposing them regularly. This makes a regular crop of the fault; and the fault becomes an established institution, and what began as a bit of carelessness ends by being a tolerated crime. Little breaches of order ought to be met by the personal authority of the teachers words and influence. If that is not enough, they should be promptly stamped out by real severity.

Inattention creeps in at another door. The operators are apt to forget the class, which is their real work, and to be absorbed in the book, and the boy doing it, whilst the rest are comparatively disregarded. The rest accord-

The operator paid in his own coin. 175 ingly are inattentive, for the operator is teaching them inattention by being inattentive to them. They are his main care, and not to care for them brings its own punishment in not being cared for. First one, then another, takes advantage of the absent eye, and disorder begins, and in spite of spasmodic severity becomes the rule. Instant, watchful, if need be, pitiless repression of the first sign of inattention is the only law of discipline. Nothing ought to escape a teacher that the boys do, for he is there to train the boys in what they do. Querulous complaints of disorder, and the inflicting of heavier, and heavier punishments,–at intervals, are the sure indication of one who forgets his duty to the class, and is inattentive to them, whilst at best he mistakes the lesson for his subject, and at worst is sleepy, capricious, and incapable himself. As mind has to be dealt with mind must be there. And however clever the performer may be, he might as well stand up, and solemnly set about giving a lesson to the clothes of the class hanging round the room on pegs, whilst the owners were playing cricket, as to the so-called class, if the boys are careless, playing, or noisy. Culpable inattention in the boys is above all things a masters fault. Able, earnest men, who attend to the class, will always find the class attend to them.

But inattention is not always wilful. There is an unconscious kind that is very dangerous, though inoffensive. Many a good, disappointed boy has been disappointed, because he has been allowed to blunder on in utter inattention when he thought he was at work, and no one has ever made plain to him the difference between sitting over his books, and an eager, intelligent love for 176 Pillows, chairs, and learners.

the work to be done. How to learn ought sometimes to be taught, and delusions about work done away with. Sleep is sleep, whether the pillow be Eschylus, or goose feathers; and sitting in the most sacred chair is not study; truths lamentably lost sight of by many a meritorious, mistaken student.

The state of mind necessary before anything can be done; the state of mind necessary whilst anything is being done will not be left out by any Teacher, who has realised that his subject is mind. The toiler and moiler ought to be plainly told, and told again, and again, the real object in view, and the preliminary processes necessary before any true work is done. Nothing is more pitiable than the spectacle of a boy spending hours of self-denial, stupefying himself by groaning over tasks unattended to, because he is groaning, and self-tortured; when all might be spared, if anyone had ever given him a lesson on the subject of his own mind, and shown him the real purpose of the work he is supposed to be doing, and how surely, and quietly it can be done. Whereas a great nightmare is on his soul, an infinity of unattainable knowledge fills all space for him. He is like one who should sit down, and mourn over the size of the world, as a reason for not Using the excellent pair of legs nature has given him for traversing that portion of it which he has to do with.

Granted however that the teacher is a teacher, and that the class knows what it is about, and is not unwilling, mere arrangement has infinite power for good or evil. A class ought to sit, or stand, compactly, under the masters eye, so that at a glance he can take in all, Inattention shops, attitude. 177 and they all are in touch with him. The moment that from the numbers, or from the structure of the room, the masters presence does not pervade the whole body, and make itself felt everywhere; if whilst speaking to one he is cut off from the many, there may be discipline, if he is a man of decision, but there will not be attention. The mechanical necessities of attention have not been complied with; an unreality, a working falsehood, has got into the work, and the work will suffer. For the same reason, no boy ought ever to sit with his back to the master, unless he is writing; in which case the paper he is writing on, and what he is doing, is in front of the eye. Still more important, if possible, is attitude. Attitude makes false work, as well as betrays false work. A competent judge shall tell in a moment by simply looking through the window where a class is at work, whether good work can be going on there. The attitude of the boys will show. For though there can be true outward observance in some degree without inward truth, the converse is not possible. There cannot be inward reality without producing an outside corresponding to it. It is a law of nature that the mind acts on the body, and makes it follow any real emotion. Everyone knows how difficult it is to restrain the outward look of anger, if angry; of sorrow, if sorrowful; and so on, through the whole range of feeling. But what is the meaning of this excepting that any reality within of necessity comes out in a corresponding bodily expression; and–that the bodily expression does show the absence of any real feeling, as well as the presence. This is a law of nature. It is equally a law of nature that every outward gesture, 178 Action of body on mind.

or expression, acts on the mind, and has a tendency to produce the inward feeling. Sir Charles Bell in his book on Expression, which every one ought to read, tells us " It is a fundamental law of our nature that the mind shall have its powers developed through the influence of the body," and he goes on to say; " How much influence the instrument of expression has in first rousing the mind into that state of activity, which we call passion or emotion, we may learn from the. power of the body to control these affections. I have often observed, says Burke, that on mimicking the looks and gestures of angry, or placid, or frightened, or daring men, I have involuntarily found my mind turned to that passion, whose appearance I endeavoured to imitate." Here is a fact for consideration, the outward gesture produced the inward feeling. A very simple experiment, so simple as to disgust all who want their prophet to come out and make a show, will convince anyone of the infinite power of this fact. There are things called arm-chairs, an ordinary upholsterer can make them. Nevertheless let a healthy person, comfortably warm, compose himself in mystic fashion in their sacred precincts, and shut his eyes, and a very few minutes sometimes will convince others, however much beyond the reach of conviction he may be himself, of the potency of attitude. The various ways in which indolent minds maltreat indolent bodies, and are dullified by them in revenge, are an approach to this somnolence, and not calculated to increase the power of coping with difficulties of learning. A Teacher will not neglect this great law of nature. Few suspect how much the waters of Helicon are contaminated by the slime which oozes in through

Attend to the body. 179 this unguarded sluice. Boys are permitted to stand up to construe with hand in pocket. And too often the slouching attitude, the sprawling, and lolling about, is enough to reveal how little is really being done within, and alas to prevent more from being done, even though the operator may be successful in turning out prize winners; but as a rule this is not the case. These are the quarters from which come complaints of the boys, of their being disorderly and inattentive, of their disregard for authority, mixed with bewailings of pains taken in vain, and querulous talking of throwing pearls before swine, varied by constant punishment, and invoking of higher authority; when all the time the operator has been disregarding laws of nature; and only had to make his class stand upright, take their hands out of their pockets, hold up their heads, and comport themselves in an intelligent way, like persons eager to learn, instead of young neer-do-weels the first Sunday they have escaped from the National School. In some instances it is a good plan to make the boy called up to construe come to a particular place as a kind of rostrum before he begins. It rouses attention, and gives an idea of the importance of the work. A system of taking places judiciously worked, and not made too much of, may be very useful in the lower classes; there is a little value in the mere fact of being on the move. A better plan still, as far as it goes, since it does not take the minds of masters, or pupils, off their work, and make the success, or failure of individuals so prominent, is the plan of making a first class, after the boys have been at work two or three weeks, and promoting and degrading those who 180 Natures revenge.

deserve it, giving some privileges to the first class as well as the honour of selection.

Finally there-is another most unfailing hot-bed of inattention, a perfect invention for growing it, more fertile even than too great numbers in a class,–the length of time spent in school. Pharaoh will have his tale of hours. And nature will have her perquisites out of them. Let any adult, however practised, however zealous, under five and twenty years of age, test himself for just one day, by an hour-glass, and try and see how long he can continue to keep up his attention at a stretch over the acquiring of new knowledge, and a sad experience will teach him, if he faithfully stops his hour-glass the moment he relaxes, how ludicrously few are the minutes during which he is actually hard at work, compared with the time he believed himself to be spending. But there is a far more rough and ready, yet sufficient, test of attention. Most people hear sermons. A unanimous verdict will be given that the mind wanders occasionally even during good sermons, eyelids have been known to droop, and contemplation to be prodigal of nods, yea there have been seen gracious men asleep, whose general appear ance scarcely betokened that ill health or exhaustion were the irresistible causes of their slumber. There have been dull sermons, and will be again; it will be confessed that the percentage of actual sleep in a dull sermon is a very appreciable quantity, a visible gauge of the condition of some of the congregation; whilst who shall pretend to calculate the invisible torpor, or wandering of mind? But it is worth considering that the dullest sermon ever preached is as the blast of a trumpet compared

How to baffle Pharaoh. 181 with misunderstood lessons to a heavy, ignorant boy, who has no belief in education, no knowledge of its aims or value, no confidence that he can get it even if it is worth having, and is only alive to the fact that he knows nothing, and hates it all. There have been also dull operators in school, as well as dull preachers in Church. How can attention be secured under such circumstances? Here then is a real problem. There is natural waste also, a kind of leakage always going on, which must be taken into account in fixing the times for study.

The problem is very real. If the times are too long, inattention is bred as in a hot-bed.

If the times are not long enough the idle boys do nothing. Time to soak, so to say, as well as time to dip, is required. Natural incapacity forbids the crowding much into a small space. Strength, and energy, and training must be there before this can be done. And they are not there; they have, if possible, to be produced. The pressure of external opinion, which judges by externals, generally demands much too long a period of compulsory attendance. This form of difficulty can be met sometimes by allowing the class to go out for ten minutes in fine weather, and ventilating the room, and their brains. Preparation of the lessons out of school, or, if in school, in a less formal way, corrects in some degree this constraint. If Pharaoh still insists on too long school hours, and relief is impossible in the matter of time and place, then graduation of the subjects, beginning with the hardest, and ending with pleasanter tasks, English poetry, for instance, is the only refuge left. Indeed this graduation always ought to be pressed into 182 Attention and masters.

service. Apparently, three quarters of an hour is the longest time that an average class can be kept at work on the same subject by a master, with advantage. It will have been plain from these few remarks, first, that attention has to be taught, and does not come by the light of nature; secondly, that there is a common-sense science of the physical and mechanical conditions necessary to secure attention; and lastly, and most of all, that attention rises or falls in the barometer in proportion to the masters ability. Inattention is a masters sin. It is a weed which above all others grows on badly farmed ground.

CHAPTER VI.

THE PRACTICE OF TEACHING.

Memory. Feed it.

Memory next claims notice as the most powerful quality in the young. Every advantage ought to be taken of this to interest them, to fill them with precious freightage, and new wonders, and material of the best kind. They ought never to be loaded, like the donkey, with salt, a heavy weight all along the road, but which melts away, and leaves an empty sack the first river that has to be crossed.

By memory is meant that strange carrying power, of which all partake, and which some have to a marvellous degree, by which the owner receives and stores up, in many instances with no effort, whatever comes within reach. It is a natural gift, born with the possessor, and in. no way dependent on his intelligent appreciation in the beginning. It is a mere cart power which holds 184 Memory and recollection.

whatever is thrown into it, even nonsense which jingles, mere sounds which run with any cadence, and in fact is the faculty of an elaborate parrot catching sounds, and by no means tied down to understanding.

This early faculty is entirely distinct from the power acquired afterwards of fixing in the mind by conscious effort, and strong interest, that which is judged worthy of being fixed. Memory in this first sense is an instinct of the young, and often passes away in that shape as the owner grows older. Whereas the strong impressions, by which the attentive mind stamps indelibly what it wishes to retain, are the result of an effort; and the necessity for that effort, and the power of making it, are the result of teaching, and can be definitely taught; the two are distinct. The natural gift is now under consideration. And the fact that the young are pre-eminently endowed with this natural gift is most important in educating the young. It simply amounts to this, that whilst the young are almost devoid of any power of connected reasoning, they are superlatively endowed with the power of receiving and collecting materials. The child has memory in childhood, reasoning power in manhood as his main life functions; like the frog, which breathes through gills in early life, and attains to lungs in its respectable years of discretion. Nature prescribes accordingly that the main business of the young is to collect material; a business which the infinite novelty of the new world not a little contributes to enliven. This determines the first great axiom, or what ought to be the first great axiom of early teaching; open Fairyland. Endeavour to delight, in-Dr Pick.

Throw open Fairyland. 185 terest, fascinate the child by judiciously supplying melodious sounds, splendid imagery, touching narratives, noble adventure, noble endurance, noble sufferings. There is a fearful theory born and bred in the quagmires of Marsh-dunceland, that nothing is learning, unless it is disagreeable, or worth having, unless it is difficult. As if the value of a building consisted in the number of the bricks which built it. Thus the high beauty of the Waverley novels, the winsome charm of ballads, the music of lyric poetry, the glorious metrical romances of Scott, the holy organ tones of immortal song, are not considered to be training because they delight. But the world is large enough to tire the strongest. The more difficulties are removed, the farther the wayfarer can get. There is no fear that a too easy progress will ever do away with the need of labour. The path wants to be smoothed not roughened. Would that a law could be passed, that no child should be taught any language but its own, as a study, before ten years old. But then another law would have to be passed, that no teacher should teach, who could not make the pupils frame their own grammar rules, by leading them to see that every necessity of grammar is but common sense applied to words. And a third law would be wanted to manufacture a supply of such teachers at once. Many other legislative feats would also be required before the possibility of doing work so intelligent could begin. Here too, as in so many other cases, the finding easier ways of doing work only means enabling a far higher standard to be reached in the infinity of work to be done. Even if it were otherwise, there is no danger that the path shall 186 Natures laws.

be all flowers, and the demand on work cease for many a year; and no danger that an idle swallowing of pleasant surface literature, which is no more sustenance than tartlets are beef, should take the place of honest food. The risks are all the other way; either lumps of rules to be of use by and by, or a thin paring of Manuals, is the diet with which the stomachs of the young are loaded. By all means let there be work. Careful selection of what has to be taken in and remembered is all that is pleaded for. Neither is the fact lost sight of that there is a grand capacity in the youthful memory of accumulating with little effort mere sounds, without understanding. This prescribes that the most useful drudgery should be got through early. And it may fairly be said, that if under present circumstances this was interpreted to mean that an absolutely infallible accuracy of declensions and conjugations was acquired, years of after toil would be saved, and in many instances lifelong incapacity be turned into healthy activity of mind. No tongue can tell the hopeless state of muddle which is produced by scrambling into the word-quagmire without a single bit of solid knowledge to rest the sole of the foot on. Nature therefore in giving the young a youthful memory lays down its own laws, if any one would heed them. First fill the great receptacle with everything that inspirits, and interests, all treasures of melodious verse, all thrilling narrative of daring deeds, all simple pathos of touching endurance, mingled with the weird, wild truths of the wonders of the animal and physical world. And secondly, all drudgery necessary to be known, which is not better learned in the practising it, word-

Bad repetition. 187 forms, and everything belonging to word-forms and their meaning, may well be stored up at once. But rules, and technical terms, should be avoided as much as possible. They pass for understanding without being understood; and not unfrequently are the cause of all the entanglement of after years; when the stock names are answered to the stock questions; and oftentimes neither teacher nor learner have the least idea of the real purport of the words they use so glibly. It is easy to learn books of rules, and never apply them. It is easy to answer them correctly and be quite ignorant why the answer is correct. Rules are the refuge of the brainless; and the instrument. of those who have to produce some show without the time or machinery necessary for true work.

This is bad enough, but there is worse behind. Bad repetition. Bad repetition is grown as a regular crop by a well-calculated system of cultivation in many instances. Nothing is more common than the setting lessons too long to be thoroughly learnt in the time allowed. This is worse than lost time. Experience shows that two different kinds of maimed power result from this, each according to the kind of victim. The slow, clumsy learner settles down into a heavy persistency that he cannot learn, and that it is no use trying to do so. Which is indeed only too true as long as a dull, unhelping hand above forces the yoke down on a dull, repugnant mind below. This process turns out the unbelievers in culture, the carnivorous stags. But the quick, clever wits acquire a fatal facility of quickly catching up. the task at the time, and forgetting it as quickly, to the permanent injury of steady, retentive grasp.

188 Lessons in inaccuracy.

But there is worse still behind. Many operators allow nonsense to be repeated; in other words, they first permit the pupil to neglect the great fact that the sense is the strongest hook to fasten the words on to the mind, and also the only thing worth fastening on; and secondly, let him go off with innumerable errors fixed in his mind instead of knowledge, as far as anything is fixed. Inaccuracy in fact is taught as a lesson.

How few apparently have any idea of instructing their pupils how to learn. The metre is neglected. In other words, that rhythmical measure, which makes the melody of poetry, and causes it to be easier to learn than prose, is allowed to go for nothing. Here again not mere for-getfulness is the evil, but inaccuracy is taught as a lesson.

Then even the correct words are mumbled in such a fashion that it matters little whether they are correct or not; all the life is gone out of them. Indifference is taught as a lesson.

Yet these points are points of teaching, and belong to a teacher. Forgetfulness would be a light evil; but unmetrical, slipshod nonsense, full of words mangled, mispronounced, ungrammatical, mere dead lumps, shapeless, and vile, all this is poured into the memory, to reappear again, and again, any number of times, in idiotic mistakes, and to form a ruinous habit of never having accurate knowledge in anything. No! forgetfulness is a blessing, when inaccuracy is taught as a lesson. Happy would many teachers be, if the pupils they receive did forget. Forgetfulness is a blessing when inaccuracy is taught as a lesson, as it must be when too much is required to be learnt.

Thoroughness a fallacy. 189

The last point of those mentioned as belonging to the minds to be dealt with is the demand for thoroughness. This properly falls under the main head of the powers of reasoning, and how far they are to be found in the young; but is so pretentious, and so frequently put forward, that a little special notice given to it will not be out of place. There is something so wise, so unanswerable, in the modest, yet firm requirement that the lessons must be done thoroughly, and a boy not advance till he has mastered what he is doing, that the request commands assent at once; there is also so real a truth underlying the dictum that the fallacy involved in it easily escapes notice. The fallacy is,–it cannot be done. There is no power in the minds of the young to master a subject thoroughly. Thorough mastery is the perfection of trained skill, and it is absurd to demand the perfection of trained skill from the untrained beginner. The map-work which transfers to the mind a complete plan of the country belongs to men; it is enough, and more than enough, if the boy can find his way about fairly well, and appreciate the landscape. Any attempt to linger too long over the same work will only end in weariness, and deadening the interest. Words and work, when stale, become to the young mere empty sounds, meaningless rote-work. There must be change. Looseness indeed is fatal. What is known ought to be known with exactness; but a gap is no harm, unless it is in the middle of the main highway. Monotony is the greatest enemy a teacher has to deal with. There is much danger, where all is new, as it is with beginners, lest a boy find a dead level without landmatks to guide. Where all is new, all i go Move on and r(p.

cannot be mastered, and in the first confusion, unless he moves on, there is nothing to show what is intended to be done, or where he is to go. This perplexity is much increased very often by indiscriminate fault finding, which instead of marking a distinct narrow path through the thicket, mixes up great and little, stumbling in the way, and wandering off the way, errors of ignorance, and errors of laziness, non-work and bad work, mental peccadilloes, and mental crimes, in one inextricable tangle from which there is no escape, because there is no clear idea whatever given to the boy mind of anything. Whereas though thoroughness is impossible, and there is far too much novelty to be mapped out, there is no impossibility whatever in marking, pioneer fashion, a track on which a boy shall feel perfectly safe. This feeling of perfect safety is the one thing no bad teacher dreams of giving, and which every good teacher makes it the first business of his life to try to impart. Again, many difficulties in learning cannot be mastered by standing still over them; they can only be got rid of by movement. They are like what happens to the traveller. In the valley, on the low ground, the fog reigns, and as long as the traveller stops in the valley, will continue to reign, not to be wrestled with, or overcome; but let him move up, and move up, and by degrees mere movement brings him into a clearer atmosphere, the mist vanishes away, and at the top of the hill the whole great landscape in all its beauty is clear, and the little hollows with their fog are mere specks, even if they still are there. So it is with the boy mind, never let it stay too long in the hollows. Movement is absolutely necessary; at the Index Expurgatorius. 191 same time the back work ought to be incessantly kept up by a small portion of time being devoted weekly to foundation work. And the teachers throughout a School ought to have an Index Expurgatorius of faults to be stamped out; each class keeping in communication with the one above, and below it, so as to waste no labour, and to be aware what the idler boys ought to know. Extreme accuracy in the structure of common sentences, and the forms of common words, ought to be universal. No good teacher allows any shortcoming here. But thoroughness in the ordinary sense of the word is impossible by the laws of nature.

CHAPTER VII.

PRACTICE OF TEACHING.

T7ic Blurred Chromograph. Sham Mistakes. Snores. Lunatic Mistakes. No Answers.

The actual teaching comes next. No words can exaggerate the importance of the first rule to be laid down.

The observance of it would revolutionise the whole world of tuition.

It is so simple that it can be observed.

So simple, that few observe it.

So simple, that those who want talk, and will do anything, and undergo anything rather than think, and act, will scorn to observe it.

Many boys, who all their lives long know nothing because of early tangle, would know.

All would save half their time.

What then is this talisman, this Columbuss egg, this simple magic and magic simplicity, this Aladdins lamp,

The blurred Chromograph. 193 which is to whisk everything into place, and create half a lifetime for all?–Articulation.–Nothing more than a rigid, absolute unfailing exacting of articulate speech, and the pronouncing the final syllable of each word firmly, distinctly, and unmistakeably.

The full force of this statement is not seen at once. It has been proved that accuracy is the first, and main object of training, both the power of accurate observation, and the power of reproducing accurately what has been observed. It has been proved also that one of the main advantages of an unspoken language as an instrument of training consists in the number of inflected forms, the changes, that is, in the final syllables. The orderly multitude of small word-labels, all calling for intelligent observation, is that property of language which makes language in the first instance such a valuable drill-master, apart from any other consideration. Every one has seen an imperfect chromograph. Let us suppose for a moment a chromograph of a book in which every final syllable was left out, or blurred, and this too in a foreign language. What would be the value of that copy to a learner with its pages full of words cut in half? Precisely the same value, that inarticulately spoken lessons are to the miserable victim, who is permitted to drop, or blur his final syllables. Add to this that the human chromograph possesses the unenviable faculty of filling in all the blurred or dropped portions incorrectly at will, and so of keeping and cherishing not a merciful blank, but a most cruel torment of endless mistakes. And all this ruinous downward training is the necessary result of inarticulate speech, and the not sounding the final 194 Sloppy minds.

syllables. A habit is formed of confusion and indecision. Confusion and indecision breed constant disappointment, in a hard-working boy especially; inaccuracy in time settles down into a conviction that nothing is certain 01 fixed, or, at least, that he cannot by any possibility arrive at it. And this in later life leads to all those sloppy theories and careless confident judgments which fill the air; and finally ends in utter and general unbelief in any one being really master of his subject; with the fitting corollary, that if no one is master of his subject, any one is at liberty to express his own views on it; and the judgment of the skilled workman is of no more account than the babble of the after-dinner talker. Nothing is a more striking sign of the rotten state of education than the absolute non-existence of any respect for the judgment of the skilled workman in his own line, whatever that line may be. Only lawyers are exempt from this irony of being handled by the amateur! The evil of inarticulate speech has much to do with this, by destroying in the great majority the sense of precision.

But to return to the learner at his task. The pupil in language might be defined in his early stages as one whose business it is to stamp on his memory the last syllable of words. Therefore he is allowed never to pronounce one of them distinctly. The blurred chromo-graph sprawls over his whole mental tablet, with an ever increasing family of mistakes, till at last in hopeless bewilderment he dubs himself utterly stupid, gives up the struggle and leaves off trying to get on, accusing his poor calumniated mind, when all the time the only culprit is his tongue, and the teacher, who has not taught him how

Snores. Sham mistakes. 195 to use his tongue properly. If articulate speech is really taught, and the accurate attention necessary for articulate speech is the habit of the room, then the next step is natural and easy. Accuracy demands that the right thing should be known, and, if known, said at once. Therefore–never allow a boy to correct himself. That is, inflict at once whatever penalty the mistake carries with it without fail; and then, and not till then, make the offender mend his ways. Or, at least, impose silence until your questions have exposed the blunder. There is a vast army of mistakes, which are no mistakes at all in the sense of being wrong mistaken for right. They are merely the loose snores of the unwaked mind; when the construer, or answerer, knows perfectly well, as well as his master does, the actual bit of knowledge to be produced, but has been permitted again, and again, to spit out what came uppermost, and–to correct it. He has not made an intelligent mistake, he has not even made an idle, unintelligent mistake, he has simply snored, emitted an unthought of sound out of a drowsy cavern of non-life. It is no mistake at all; as he proves the next moment, and very often will admit, by correcting it promptly and with ease. No correction ought ever to be allowed to avert blame, or penalty. This rule does not interfere with that most useful of all minor inflictions, the pushing an idle, careless boy through the bit he is maltreating, forcing him to flounder on, to sprawl about, to take every word, and render each, as he takes them, however absurdly, in all the hideous deformity of words unknown, grammar defied, and sense nowhere; and then when he has finished, reading out the result. There is 196 Guesses, snap shots.

no worse fault in teacher or taught than not keeping close to the work, and working with certainty. Real mistakes are one thing. Sham mistakes are another. And the learners ought to have the distinction sharply and strongly cut across their minds. A boy ought to be made to see always that what he can do he shall do. Faults of ignorance are very real, and faults of idleness are very real, but at any given moment there may be great difficulty, nay, impossibility, of judging whether any blame or punishment is deserved by the guilty, but unfortunate creature, who has made them. But sham mistakes admit of no such doubt; they are unpardonable; and if every teacher agreed in never allowing this preventable crime; never allowing a correction; never allowing these senseless snores to pass; a great revolution would be effected. It is not the knowledge of the miserable Tense, or Case, that is the question, but the slackness of mind that is so deadly, the trained activity that is at stake. Sham mistakes should be exterminated promptly. They are mere vacuity, total absence of training and thought.

There are many varieties of the sham mistake.

Guessing pure and simple is akin to this absence of thought. The snorer and the guesser are twins. "Both thrive under bad teaching." "Common mistakes," writes one, "are those due to wild guessing. A boy takes a shot, as the question goes by, on the chance of getting up. Hence a verb may have twenty different Perfects and Supines given it as it goes down the class." What a graphic picture! Twenty boys with necks outstretched, eagerly gasping at their chances of making

Lunatic mistakes. 197 mistakes–in ofder to be promoted, and–the serene power in the clouds above permitting it. This is only too faithful a sketch of what is done, and ought not to be done. The artist has depicted with fidelity, from the life, the native simplicity of English teaching. But the guesser can easily be brought to book Let him be told to look steadily at the questioner, and be asked, what boy, or tree, or picture, or whatever may be there, inside or outside the room, is behind his back; and be bantered when he cannot tell, and be bid guess, and laughed at for not guessing, and when he has been made sufficiently uncomfortable, be shown how utterly idiotic it is to make a guess at what he knows nothing about, with the range of the whole world for his guesses to disport in, when he cannot even guess what is close to him, and one of the few things that can be near him.

Next there is a distinct class of sham mistakes which may be called lunatic mistakes. The following dialogue will explain what is meant. A bit of stray nonsense is turned loose by a boy.

Master. Are you deaf?

Boy. No.

M. Are you blind?

B. No.

M. An idiot?

B. I dont think so.

M. Just imagine then that we two are out walking, and meet a dog. I say "look at that calf." What do you do?

B. Say its a dog, it isnt a calf.

M. What! contradict the Headmaster?

tgs The Lunatic asylum.

B. A dogs a dog. I must, because it is a dog.

M. What! venture to know better than the Headmaster?

B. I cant help it. It is a dog.

M. Well. To take another case, say 2 x 2 = 5.

B, But it doesnt.

M. What! contradicting again?

B. Yes, of course, I must.

M. Suppose I persist in saying it is 5?

B. You would be mad.

M. What 1 you able to judge that I was mad?

B. Why! yes.

M. Well, lets move on. Genitor is the genitive case.

B. But it isnt.

M. Contradicting the Headmaster again?

B. I cant help it.

M. Well then, 2x2 = 5 and Genitor the Genitive case are as much signs of madness in me and you as calling a dog a calf?

B. Yes, certainly they are.

M. All I can say is we have made a most interesting discovery this morning. This is a most flourishing Lunatic Asylum. Not a day passes in which dogs and calves are not jumbled in beautiful confusion and perfect indifference as to which, by you and your companions. Many of these things you know quite as well as I do, if you would but stick to what you know. It is not true that you are ignorant. You have already a considerable amount of real, solid knowledge under your feet, on which you rtan stand firmly, and advance firmly, without sticking in the mud, or tumbling into ditches!

Quagmire got rid of. 199 In this way that most important point may be established in a boys mind that he does know something, and can gain positive knowledge. He can be made to feel in himself that his mind can deal with work; that it is not all quagmire, floating, unstable, treacherous, unsavoury stench, hateful in his nostrils, and useless. It is impossible to overrate the importance of giving confidence. Very much of what is called idleness, and inattention, is only utter bewilderment, produced by the unsystematic way in which the swarm of novelties has been thrust on the beginner; and the unsystematic way in which technical Terms, Tense, Mood, Case, andc. which he does not know the meaning of, have been crammed into him; and the unsystematic way in which rules, which are pure Chinese to him, have been substituted for teaching; and the unsystematic way in which praise and blame, alike unintelligible, have been poured over him; till drenched, eyes and nose full, blinking and dazed, he is left the fortunate owner of a few answers by rote to the more familiar questions as the reward for hours of disgust and toil.

As a further corrective to this drenching process, a boy ought never to be permitted to answer any question but the one he is asked.

E. g. if a boy says vicerunt, and the master asks, What did you say? the boy must be made to answer vicerunt, and not allowed to correct it to vicerunt. This necessitates too, that a master should be very careful what he does ask, and should keep watch upon himself as well as over his pupils.

The inflexible rigidity of words when once written 2OO Rigidity of words.

should be impressed on learners. This it is which makes mistakes lunatic. Whilst on the other hand, the almost infinite variety of ways in which thought can be clothed in words without greatly altering the sense tends to make a beginner confound the two, and play tricks with the words, which when once put out are inflexible. Because the translation may be very different in construction and yet right, they assume that the original words may be turned topsy-turvy with impunity. This is a very dangerous snare. No beginner ought ever to be allowed to give a rendering however good, unless he has first given the literal version, and kept to the grammatical shape of the original, however un-English it may be. And no master ought ever to be deluded into giving the boys better words, until he is sure that they know the exact sense and the literal rendering. Otherwise all the wild vagaries of guessing, and snoring, and lunatic mistakes, are simply bred, and cultivated as a natural growth from such planting.

In like manner, for it is part of the same aimless straggling, no commoner fault occurs than the no answer at all, e. g. the master asks "What case is tempora?" The ordinary boy as likely as not says, "It is a noun." Very true, but that is no answer. It cannot be too sternly impressed on boys that there are only two kinds of answers, a right answer, and a wrong answer. The no-answer plague is always breaking out, and furnishes a very good test of the kind of teaching that is going on. Yet it is very difficult even for a good teacher to get rid of it, unless there is much vigilance on all sides, and careful explanation of why things are wrong, and what is

Elaborate anarchy. 201 being aimed at. As long as hazy ideas of knowledge, and accumulation, and the shop full, rule the world, so long it is vain to expect boys or teachers to escape from these epidemics. Probably, much of this will appear childish, much unpractical, to readers, who would infinitely prefer a finer and more intellectual brain-spun web. They will say to themselves, This is nonsense, these things do not occur, or rarely; and if they do, a few days will stamp them out. What bad teachers are supposed, and what absurdly bad pupils! Thirty years of practical experience of all kinds enable one to lay down that this is not childish, absurd, or overdrawn, but very sober, everyday fact. Every day is increasing instead of diminishing the evil. If the teachers are bad, and the pupils are bad, what will they be fifty, or a hundred years hence, when the present elaborate anarchy has matured its weeds? Thirty years ago every one did what was right in his own eyes, there was wrong-doing on all sides, but nothing was fixed. There was possibility of reform. Since then Jupiter has sent us down a Pandora, and missed Hope out of her box; now we sin by law, and boast as we rattle our chains.

CHAPTER VIII.

THE PRACTICE OF TEACHING.

Run the Goose down.

The questions hitherto discussed have belonged pretty equally to teacher and taught; and pertain to the outward form and manner of working. But there are a number of things also belonging to the form of the work which exclusively belong in the first instance to the masters and teachers and only reach the taught through them.

A Teacher, as has been mentioned earlier, ought to make a definite scheme in his own mind, and enter it in his private memorandum book;, according to which he works day by day, and keeps to the path, never losing sight of the track. If this is not done he will wander at random at the beck of every new difficulty, and rush off anywhere as the mistakes of the day blindly occur, and attract his attention. And his class will rush off in like

Run the goose down. 203 manner, scattering in brainless confusion. Many a Master runs about mentally just as if he was trying to catch geese on a common. There is the flock assembled in a reasonably compact body. He makes a dash into the middle, of course missing his victim; and off they go in all directions, he after them, first chasing one, then another, till the flock has ceased to be a flock, and he, all out of breath, is no longer within reach of any of them. Run one goose quietly into a corner, run him down, is the first rule of catching geese; and a good rule too, whether in class room, or on common. Every fault must not be chased. A very few days will show what elementary mistakes of ignorance, or carelessness, the boys are in the habit of making. Let them be noted, and a gradual scale privately written down, beginning with the most elementary. As soon as this is done the Teacher is in a position to formally open the campaign. The lessons proceed with varied fortune day by day; but the Teacher merely corrects all other mistakes, and lays down the law himself briefly, not spending time on any of them, still less wasting good wrath, but he fastens on any of the two or three faults he is determined to get rid of. He hammers at them during part of every lesson, and gives serious notice to nothing else in the way of mistakes, or bad work. Like the great Alexander, "He fights his battles over again, and thrice he slays the slain." For they need it, they have an awkward trick however often their throats are cut of reappearing again.

The boys in this way learn the distinction between serious faults, and faults of pardonable ignorance; the 204 Classification of faults.

briar-patch begins to have a path in it. They learn to see that amidst the apparently infinite throng of novelties and difficulties they are only required to take them one by one. Like the never-to-be forgotten story of the discontented clock, they find out that however many millions of seconds have to be ticked, only one is wanted at a time, and with this discovery much of the terror of work vanishes. Obviously the same plan must be pursued in what has to be hammered in, as well as in what has to be hammered out. In fact the one properly done is the other. Extend this principle, and suppose that the Teachers throughout the school are working in unison on this plan, and, well! a new creation will have begun. But even in the case of the single Teacher, however unsupported on either side, this simple process absolutely alters the whole climate, lifts the fog off the work, sweeps clear the foggy mind, and the foggy field of labour equally. Nothing conduces to clearness and accuracy so much as a careful classification of fault-finding. The simple rule, "fix on your goose, and run him down," is of marvellous practical power.

Again, much help can be given towards simplifying work, and lessening the apparent infinity of it. In that way also the goose can be run down. The fact that between eighty and ninety per cent, of the words in an ordinary Latin author are found in English has already been mentioned. But what a fact that is! To say nothing of the use of thus knowing your own language (and who can tell how much language-power would be lost if this was given up), a complete and absolute transformation takes place in the work itself; the learner,

The word-army, its uniforms. 205 instead of being landed in a foreign country, helpless, and penniless, amongst strangers, finds himself a kind of detective policeman being trained to find out old friends in disguise. Much interest can be roused in this way, at the same time that the endless labour shrinks into very modest dimensions. It is well also to reduce the sentence difficulty in the same manner to itsdue proportions by showing, that every sentence in the world from the first spoken words to the last must have the same skeleton of Subject and Predicate, Noun and Verb, with their belongings. This cannot change, but must always be there in one shape or another. So that if a boy is taught to grasp firmly the main bone, and put the sentence together bit by bit, instead of going at it all at once, the goose is run down here too.

There is a still more remarkable simplification even than this, which a Teacher can draw attention to. The vast number of words frighten the learner. But let no time be lost in making a boy see that the more there are the easier it is to know their duties. To take an illustration. The words are as an army, divided into regiments. The meaning of each word is the soldiers name, but the badges produced by inflexion are the uniform of each regiment. The more men in a regiment, the easier to recollect their uniform. In an army of 100,000 men it would be a great feat for a commander, or any one, to know all their names; in like manner to know the meaning of every word in the language under treatment is hard. But then they are not wanted to be known all at once, and this fact should be made plain. On the other hand, the uniform see tten; 206 Picking up dropped stitches.

seen ten times, it has more chance of being remembered; seen ten thousand times no one can help knowing it. But this is true in the word-army; the more verbs there are conjugated like amo, the easier it is for anyone to remember words conjugated like amo, that is, if he ever really knew amo. Alas, a sad experience proves that this preliminary step is very often not taken, and that in the bustle, confusion, and press of this non-teaching generation the whole creaky cranky factory-chimney of tumbledown knowledge owes its utter want of stability in a great degree to the very simple fact of being founded on a sand-heap, of nothing ever having been really learned, no, not even the parrot work done in good style. When at a later period this is discovered, hopeless as it seems at first sight, and in some measure is, yet there is a partial remedy. Teachers often err from doing nothing, unless they can do it in a regular way, with much expenditure of time. Very often much can be done, and very little time expended. Five minutes given each lesson time to picking up dropped stitches will effect wonders. A little special attention during preparation time in pointing out to a rickety boy the particular points in the lesson he should pay most attention to is another great means of under-pinning the superstructure. But above all adapting the exercises in composition to the defects to be corrected in a boy, works powerfully towards pulling the pieces together, and making something like order in the mind.

The same policy can be pursued in a more general way. Every good Teacher after he has spent the regulation time in doing the regulation lesson, hearing the

Non-official work. 207 construing, and questioning the grammar in and out of the class, will from time to time spend the last five minutes, or so, in telling the class himself, whilst they listen, such information, grammatical, or other, which he thinks likely to be most effective. This gives every Teacher in a right way, and on a definite plan, the opportunity of throwing some of his own life into the work going on, and casting a gleam of light, yea of very sunshine, on to the heaviest ploughed field of stick-in-the-mud clay. He can make a great man a living presence, or a daring deed breathe fire, or the dim battles of kites and crows, as it were, lose their vague unreality, and step out bold and free again, man struggling with man, and life and death, the life and death of men and nations hanging on the issue. This kind of non-official work again enables a Teacher to illustrate all the work done in the strange language, by the familiar examples of our own tongue; and thus connect both the meaning of the words and the structure of the sentences with daily life. He explains why the languages seem to differ, and what is the loss or gain in English as compared with Latin or Greek. Living interest is thrown into the language lesson by this, and the dullest can be made to see that he is not engaged in a disgusting, nor unprofitable study, but that it is worth his while to do it, though he may find it difficult.

Following this same track, the Teacher throughout every class in the school ought once a week to read and explain to his class such an author as they can follow, be it English, or Latin, or Greek, according to their capacity. This is calculated to give a taste for literature, 208 Weekly lectures.

and to provide a good deal of material at a small expenditure of time. At all events it breaks the chains of necessary routine, and lets a master loose, if he has any real feeling or life in him, to cultivate in some degree what he likes best, and bring it in as part of his school work. This can be a source of as much fresh life to him as to his class, and may be made a most real link between the teacher and the taught. Again nothing is more felt in the present day, the moment any attempt is made to train each boy, be he clever or stupid, than the ignorance that is disclosed. No sooner does a search begin into the boys minds, than carnivorous stags, cantering whales, and four-legged dolphins are found rampaging in all directions; and the daily tasks, with the tale of bricks rigidly demanded by Pharaoh, bring no hope of anything better. They simply leave the whole matter of ignorance in common objects on one side, absolutely untouched. This is a very baffling difficulty. Yet if during one Term in the year, one afternoon a week is set apart for a Lecture to the whole school on any subject whatever worth lecturing on, much general knowledge of common but unknown things can be given, grand battues of carnivorous stags, and other such game, take place, interest be excited, and freshness poured into the school routine. Not the least valuable part of this plan is the advantage it is to the Masters themselves. Has any one of them a Hobby, a favourite pursuit, he is able to bring it out, and air it before an appreciative audience, to exhibit, himself as a human being with human sympathies, and not merely a mummified paste of Greek and Latin verbs. Lecturers and able men not on the staff of the

Lectures.

209 school can also be called in in a natural way to help the work, and the sphere of power available very much enlarged in consequence. All this belongs to masters, and is their work. A Teacher is not a Teacher who neglects these various forms of training life.

CHAPTER IX.

THE PRACTICE OF TEACHING.

Playing with the bat upside down.

The boys do not know how to set about learning, they ought to be taught. This teaching cannot be given through the medium of the unknown. It will be acknowledged that the power to observe a simple thing, note the actual facts first, and then return the plain answers which the actual facts give out, or suggest, is the very beginning of mental training. For a plain answer to a plain question means a plain view of a fact seen by the mind. It is the business of teaching to give this plain view. For learning is not necessarily the same as being taught; any more than losing your way is the same as getting quickly to your journeys end. Learning may mean getting knowledge anyhow; whereas being taught means applying mind with skill, and understanding how to apply mind. There

Observe, picture, answer. 211 s is as definite a machinery for arriving at right answers, as w there is for building a house. But the boys do not know ei this; they neither observe, nor picture, nor answer. a That is, they do not know the process by which it is done; and piling in new difficulties (what is called learning is very often this, and nothing more), naturally does not help them. They ought to be taught. It is the beginning of true knowledge to know how to learn. It is not the intention of this treatise to give technical instruction, but only to suggest ways of working. Nevertheless in this instance ways of working can scarcely be suggested without giving a slight sketch and examples in outline of what is meant. Let the teacher, for instance, of an ordinary class ask the boys to give an account of any well-known object, say, an apple. Whats an apple? Minutes on minutes will be spent before any reasonable description of it will be given. Nevertheless however different the powers of the boys may be for putting into words a really vivid and accurate account of an apple, there is a most definite machinery for enabling the mind to set about answering rightly, which every boy in the class ought at once to put in action. This is given more at length in the Schoolboys Chapter; it will be sufficient to observe here that the moment the question is asked every boy ought to picture to himself the thing mentioned in as many aspects as possible; to have it actually before his eye, if he can, and examine it; if he cannot, to see it in his minds eye, really see it, take each part, one by one, compare it with the things most like it, and then note the peculiar facts which make it different from everything else. But there will not be a single boy out of 212 The machinery of answers.

hundreds, who may be questioned in this way, who has ever had this quiet bit of teaching given him; which is mere machinery, the machinery of every right answer in the world, and quite as mechanical an instrument of mind for playing the mind game, as a bat is for playing cricket, and quite as independent of the powers of the player. It has nothing to do with the strength, or weakness, ignorance, or knowledge of the boys, it simply has to do with the external fact of their using their instrument in the right way, or not. It is impossible to lay too much stress on the machinery process by which every question in the world that is rightly answered is brought to the right answer, consciously or unconsciously. Can a teacher be a teacher who does not teach this?

To take a second example somewhat more complex than the apple! " The sower went forth to sow his seed." If a really intelligent answer is to be given as to the meaning of the word " seed" under such circumstances, the process is, first to picture in the mind a seedsmans shop with all its various seeds, none better to the eye than another, hard dry facts all of them, and to contrast it with the summer garden, where every flower and plant declare what they are, self-revealed. The main distinctions of the seed stand out at once. Next the seed must be pictured in the ground, all its hard dry nature vanishing, it is full of new movement, roots penetrating in subtle, tender shapes of change, and as they change, drawing the secret powers of the ground into fresh vitality, the seed thus growing with a growth of its own, and so on. All this kind of truth and power of answer proceed to a very great extent by rule, the very

Sense determines construction. 213 simple rule of at once picturing the object named, con-trasting it with its nearest neighbours, and noting the peculiarities, which present themselves as things seen, rather than as researches of thought.

To apply this to words. What is the construction of the word "when" we will ask. This is only another form of asking, what is the real meaning of the word "when"? The meaning of the word " when" can only be discovered by framing sentences to show its meaning. A little trouble will make it clear that the word " when " in such a sentence as, " when the end has come, all is over," means, " the moment the end has come all is over"; and again, in the sentence, " when he was in India he hunted," that the word " when" means, " at various uncertain times." Nothing can be more different than these two meanings; and accordingly the constructions used will be very different in every language in which shades of mood are marked. Whenever the word " when" means the exact moment, an Indicative or Fact-mood must be used; and whenever " when " means a floating moment, the Conjunctive or Thought-mood must be used. But the finding out the meaning of " when " proceeds by rule, the very simple rule of at once picturing to the mind the two kinds of sentences by which the two kinds of meaning are made to stand out in visible relief. Again, exactly the same rule is applicable to innumerable sentences, and difficulties of sentence structure. For example, " would old age be less burdensome if they were passing their eight hundredth year, rather than their eightieth," What is the construction of the end of the sentence? The moment 214 Examining nothing.

it is filled in the construction is evident, viz. " less burdensome than it would be, if they were passing their eightieth year." Or again, let the sentence in Shakespeare be taken, "If it were farther off Ill pluck it down." There can be much confusion in getting an account of this sentence, which presents no difficulty at all, as soon as the suppressed clauses are filled in, viz. " If it were farther off, / should pluck it down, and however far off it is, I will pluck it down." Sight, so to say, supplies the place of thought, as soon as a few plain instructions are given as to how to learn. The fact is, it is impossible to examine and report on–nothing: and until attention is drawn to this, much time is wasted in examining and reporting on–nothing. The beginner has no definite object before his minds eye, and till he is taught the plain common-sense rule that he must have a definite object before him, and is shown how to have a definite object before him, he has not learnt how to set about his work.

Lastly, let a narrative be taken, and subjected to the same treatment, in order to show how the principle should be applied. Probably history does not furnish any better known or more touching picture than the raising of the daughter of Jairus. Now the machinery of the narrative, viewed as a subject of study, is twofold, ist, there are the main pictorial facts, and their translation into modern life and practice; 2ndly, there are the minor pictorial facts, and their translation. The main pictorial facts are as follows: i. The hot Eastern sun shining on the sea shore with its open space, and room for the great multitude to stand round our Lord.

The machinery of narrative. 215 2. The crowd of fishermen, townspeople, and strangers at the little sea-port.

3. Our Lord teaching all these people, who were eager to hear Him.

4. The principal man of the place in great sorrow interrupting this popular meeting.

5. Our Lord at once for an act of mercy leaving the shore, breaking off His important work, and in spite of the heat, and the crowd, going into the narrow close streets of the town.

6. The crowd following, much jostled in the narrow streets, so thronged that they could not help pushing, but so respectful that the poor invalid woman was able to get through them, and reach the Lord.

7. The poor, pale sufferer coming up.

8. The delay, and the fathers anxiety, and the impatience and curiosity of the crowd.

9. The fine house of Jairus, the crowd forced to wait outside, the mourners within, and their noise, and the chamber of death, and the solemn restoration from the dead.

These are the main pictorial facts which a class ought to see. Then translated into modern life they suggest of themselves excitement that calls itself reli. gious; curiosity of all kinds, but outwardly religious also: the followers who think themselves doing a favour by following; apparent zeal, real inconvenience, mixed motives, people judging for good or evil, the spectators and their feelings, with all the busy self-importance both of those who join, and those who dont join in the movement; and a thousand images of disturbance, and cha- 216 Translating facts.

racter, round a religious centre, but far from religious, as well as the deep central truth of Christ present, and of life in the great sorrow of the father.

Then the minor facts are ist. The delay and its incidents.

andly. The mourners, and the scene in, and round the house.

3rdly. The request of the father to the Lord " to come and lay His hands on the child," and the idea of the woman, that it was necessary to touch Him.

4thly. The value of interruptions.

There is no need of dwelling on these and like facts, or even translating them into modern life, enough has been shown as a sample, yet it may be worth while drawing attention, as a bit of pictorial teaching, to the entirely inadequate, not to say wrong views, of Jairus and the woman with regard to the Lords Person and Power, which our Lord at once accepts, and acts on; whilst thousands of Christians spend their whole lives in wrangling over, upholding, or rebuking, imperfect views of doctrine or sacraments, and sometimes furiously deny all salvation to those who think too much or too little of the touch, and the hem of the garment.

This however is an example of the machinery of teaching, and is not intended to go into minute detail, but only to show in an ordinary narrative what machinery process has to be set going consciously or unconsciously, consciously however if there is any teaching, in order to present the subject in such a manner as may bring out its real knowledge.

Years of useless toil might be saved if the learners

Answered but not learnt, 217 only knew how to set about their work. Many other devices to make learning skilful and effective will occur to the practical teacher, but, as this is not a teachers manual, it is sufficient to point the way. What things the attention ought to be fixed on, and in what way, what to forget, and what to remember, unobtrusive peculiarities that require notice, obtrusive excellences that stick of themselves, these, and many like instructions, which experience suggests, can shorten labour, and cause time to be employed to the best advantage. But even to draw attention to the science of learning, and the intelligent skill, that can exist, and may be imparted, in the process of setting to work intelligently will be a wondrous advance. As yet the boy world, at all events, knows nothing of it.

Again, there is another aspect of the not-having-been-taught-to-learn question. No one, who has not examined his own class on the work of the past term, and had continued, aye, long-continued experience, could possibly believe, that a teacher might spend weeks and weeks in laying down a few principles of work, and questioning in and out of the boys a few elementary beginnings of intelligent treatment of sentences, and–have those questions answered,–and yet at the end find that no single boy had paid any real attention; and that the work had all to be done over again. If this is the case, as it is, with the most carefully worked-out plan, what happens when there is no plan at all, and a mere farmers-wife scattering represents the work of the operator, and a punishment lottery the condition of the boys? The fact is, the sole idea of work thr– 218 The meaning of teaching unknown.

many good boys have is the filling the knowledge shop; and the work they do themselves is their only idea of the process. It never enters their minds that the teacher is there not to correct mistakes, hear lessons, and show them word-tricks, and examples of successful work, but to point out the way in which they ought to prepare their minds for doing any work at all. And as this never enters their minds, they naturally reject it even when it is done, and like a bad player of a familiar game, are only conscious of their misses and hits, and superbly blind to the wrong attitude, and the clumsy position, which the scientific player knows will leave them comparative failures to the end of time. The art of learning has no existence for them, and they cannot see that they ought to readjust their crooked, selfwilled mental postures at the teachers word; that is not their idea of being taught, and they cannot bring themselves to receive it. They will not take it. This is a very serious evil. Bad work is one thing. But working in the wrong way is another. Every teacher, who is a teacher, ought to draw a strong distinction between faults of ignorance, which may be pardonable, and faults of refusing to be taught, and persisting in doing things the wrong way in spite of teaching. A sharp, unmistakeable line ought to be drawn between the two. The class ought never to be able to confound for one moment the not doing what they can do, and are shown how to do daily, with any mistake however gross and startling, which is of ignorance however culpable. But the misfortune is, the mistakes are gross and startling, they get up and hit the master as it were in the face, whilst the refusing to be

Play with the bat upside down. 219 taught is silent, and a planless master does not observe it at all, and accordingly it often escapes scot-free.

Nevertheless working in the wrong way is playing the game with the position wrong, cricket with the bat held upside down, no play at all–and never will be play. Bad work is clumsy cricket, which may improve in time. The fact that there is a right way and a no-way, ought to pervade the whole school life from end to end always. Every teacher ought to know how he is teaching, and how his neighbours are teaching, and never permit play with the bat upside down. Some examples will illustrate this, and mark the difference between bad work, and the wrong way.

When a Repetition lesson has to be said, a boy who cannot say it, and stops, and requires prompting, does bad work; and it ought to be dealt with as bad work. But if he goes on regardless of sense, violates the metre, repeats words that are non-existent, or mispronounced, or mangled, he is not working in the right way, his bat is upside down, he is not playing the game, and at that rate never will play the game. Perhaps the commonest fault of this kind is for a boy calmly to get up, and proceed to construe undiluted nonsense. This is generally treated as not knowing the lesson, and punished accordingly. But in essence, it has nothing to do with not knowing the lesson. Not knowing the lesson is ignorance, idle ignorance perhaps; but this unblushing outpour of nonsense is being a fool, a very different matter. The man of Thessaly, who was so wondrous wise, apparently did not know his way, but that was no excuse for his jumping into a bramble bush 22O The boy of Thessaly.

and scratching out both his eyes. That was being a fool. It was a waste of time, even if he knew that he could scratch them in again. But the boy of Thessaly, though quite as ready to plunge into any number of quickset hedges, does not scratch his eyes in again, but only blinds himself the more. This folly, unblushing, and common as it is, is not because the boys are fools, or shameless, but bears witness to their never having been taught that thought is the first thing, thought the second thing, thought the third thing to be learnt. It bears witness to heaps of knowledge having been presented to them to collect, however dead the lump might be; it bears witness to no one having stamped on their minds the distinction between bad play, and playing with the bat upside down.

Another common example of the total absence of mind, and the not knowing how to learn, because of the knowledge-lump theory, is this.

When something more than usually silly has been written, or said, the culprit quite unabashed defends his outrage by the portentous plea, "I found it in the dictionary." What a frightful revelation of incapacity! and alas! of never having been taught. The poor victim betrays that instead of looking on his work as a wrestling ground to win sense in, and working by the sense, struggling, if it is a struggle, into the meaning of the passage, his only conception is a hunt for words quite unconnected with thought, or sense. It has not dawned on him that ordinary life and the faculties by which he knows a cow from a horse have anything to do with what he is about; or that the great writings, which have come

Shut doors, false labels. 221 down some thousands of years to us, have anything to do with readable matter. " I found it in the dictionary!" The words are only made to be declined, and conjugated; and the whole duty of boy is summed up in the magic formula, "I found it in the dictionary." The knowledge-lump heresy is at the bottom of this. But brainless work ought to be shamed even more than brainless idleness. Brainless idleness has probably played a game when he ought to have worked, and has got something for his time; but brainless work, poor lunatic, has been occupied in burying his mind under heaps of rubbish, which he piles up laboriously, instead of clearing it away.

Another most unsuspected form of nonsense, perhaps the most deadly of all, arises from the use of technical terms, tense, number, case, mood, ando. Technical terms, when worked up to, thoroughly understood, and constantly kept fresh, are most useful in moderation, but when merely given as names to beginners, most pernicious. They are generally used for years without the least idea of their real meaning, and are taught and accepted as satisfactory answers by masters who know half their meaning, when the boy answering, who does not know their meaning at all, might just as well for all purposes of mind have called out abracadabra. They pretend to be knowledge, and are like shut doors proudly labelled " Museum," which if any daring explorer opens, he finds behind nothing but cobwebs and dust, and the door-keeper asleep with the key in his pocket. It is a strange comment on the absence of reference to mind in dealing with the young, that grammar, which is only 222 English or Chinese.

intelligent common sense applied to fix common talk, bristles with technical terms, and arbitrary rules; whereas all the ordinary structure of a sentence, and the reasons for each bit, can easily be questioned out of very young children without any book at all by a good questioner; and they can be made to frame the rules for themselves, and be their own grammarians.

After what has been said the worst fault of all those which the modern teacher has to meet is no longer incredible. It is a fault, which pervades the highest as well as the lowest class.

It is almost impossible to get the learners to take the English they ha e to deal with, and in any way attempt to get at its real meaning. The actual sense of their own language is utterly uncared for; nay, nothing is resisted so obstinately as the effort to make them grapple with the common meaning of common English sentences, which they are required to translate into Latin. If anything was wanted to prove the total absence of even beginning to apply mind in many, who have attained to considerable proficiency in rotework and practice, this refusal to get below the surface of their own language sufficiently to understand its real meaning would more than establish the painful truth. A few examples shall be quoted to explain what is meant by this, otherwise no one would comprehend the actual vacuum that has to be constantly taken account of. They are not quoted to raise a laugh, but as melancholy proof of the total absence of right ideas how to work, and desperate resistance to being put in the right way.

Idiotic genius. 223

A piece of poetry on Hellas contained the line,

"Her airs have tinged thy dusky cheek."

A boy of 18 rendered it

"Helladis heredes palida illius ora colorant."

What must have been the habitual void of all intelligent training, which could allow such inanity. The well-known version of condimenta for the Seasons belongs to this category, being begotten of " I found it in the dictionary" and disregard of the English. The well-known line of Longfellow,

"But has one empty chair,"

after passing through the cavity where a boy of 17 kept what he called his brain, reappeared as

"Qui non jejunum prope sedile tenet."

Whilst the equally wrong, but less producible mistakes of not finding out, whether such an expression as "The expedition sailed " means " the ships " or the " sailors," or, " the explorers " or " the army" simply swarm. These illustrations, and any number might be supplied, reveal a far more serious state of things than mere ignorance. It is clear that the absence of any idea of sense in the work to be done is an imported evil. It is not natural for the young to imagine, when they are in places of teaching, to which they are sent from home for the purpose of being taught, that all is nonsense, and that it is not their business to learn to use sense intelligently, or a teachers business to show them how to do so. This is the result of artificial causes; and is not produced in one generation. The fact is plain. If challenged it can 224 Unbelief in training.

be proved by endless examples, coming from all manner of different quarters, and extending over years of experience. But no one will challenge it who has attempted to teach each boy, and noted the state of things as a matter of serious thought, and not from the purely ridiculous side.

The ordinary schoolboy has no conception of coming to school to learn the right way of employing sense. The idea of intelligent mind being the subject of all school work is banished from school. It is not in the school horizon.

The daily work of every school furnishes abundant proof of this absence of mind, and mind training, and the waste of life consequent on it.

Ignorance is natural, but unbelief in training is a cultivated crop. Some of the reasons have been suggested.

Tand 5 oxXa aiya, j3oos irl yb. uaaq /ityas
, or/cos 8" 01)7-65 el (t 0oyyijv dpot
av Wec, us kui yw niisa Kot /moavffi

A schoolmaster has a prescriptive right, readily accorded him by the scornful, to be a pedant, and quote Greek.

CHAPTER X.

THE PRACTICE OF TEACHING.

Quis custodiat ipsos custodes 1

Nothing has been said about the Masters.

The writer is a Master, and knows their difficulties too well.

No scientific man has ever yet been found to dissect himself.

But as long as Teaching is impossible there can be no Teachers.

CHAPTER XI.

THE PRACTICE OF TEACHING.

Thought governs Words.

A Few words on the actual work done in the upper Schools may not be out of place. If there was a rigid railway of right with lines laid down, as there is in mathematics and in every scientific subject which has advanced beyond the range of the prophetic faculty, nothing would require to be said, as the manner in which it was taught would be the only question. But there is no such rigidity in language and literature. Language is the expression of thought, and however rigid the words once written, or spoken are, and indeed then they are fixity itself, thought can be expressed in ten thousand ways, and there is infinite choice even in the same language as to how it shall be expressed in any given instance. As soon as two languages are taken into consideration, or more, a completely new set of conditions is introduced,

The chisel and the axe. 227 and new forms of difficulty arise, according to the character of the languages which are the practice ground of training. A language with many subtle shades of meaning denoted by many slight changes of word-form will naturally be full of such subtleties; whereas a language with no such power of expressing subtle meaning by inflexion will as far as possible get rid of them. What is to be done by teacher and learner, when they are brought face to face with the fact that the same thought is put out in a very different way, whilst nevertheless it is necessary to show that in each language the way is the right way? If a literal version is given, then it is not English. If a literal version is not given, the Latin sentence is quite changed. Is there no clue? no principle which will always act in spite of the diversity? or is all chance and knack? How can the different instruments be made to do the same work? For the instruments are as different as a chisel and an axe. The first great point to observe is, that the thought governs the expression, and causes certain words to be used in a certain way; and that the words do not govern the thought. Perhaps nothing in all the Teaching world has been so fatally untrue as the treating the words of the great writers as if they decided the sense, instead of looking at the thought to be expressed, and seeing that the thought decides what words are used. Grammarians have dealt with language as if it was a game of chess, in which the words were the pieces, and every piece had a given function, and the pieces made the game, according as a skilful player moved them by rule. Whereas language is a game of life, in which thought, that is, living power, takes 228 Thought commands words.

shape in words, chooses such words as give the shape required, and then sends them into the battle-field, in well-disciplined companies to obey orders, and wheel and charge in disciplined ranks indeed, but in a thousand evolutions as the commander commands. The chess theory, in which the words are masters, is stereotyped in the most erroneous term that was ever invented, that one word governs another. This marvellous bit of Topsyturvy, has done more to turn language teaching topsyturvy than anything else in the world; and introduces inextricable confusion into the language world. As long as one word governs another, and the words are lords paramount, there is no escape from the dilemma mentioned above of two languages expressing the same thought, each in its own way, differently. But the moment the thought is accepted as the commander in chief, then it becomes plain that the thought in each instance selects an appropriate expression, and when the cause is the same, the same appropriate expression always; and the reason why it does so is known, and if any deviation is necessary, that is known also, and can be managed. To proceed then to the work.

It falls naturally under three heads:

How to Construe,

How to Translate,

How to do original Composition. How to Construe needs little to be said about it; Construing, strictly so called, requires the learner to show that he knows the exact sense, and proper grammatical construction of each word in the language he is construing from, and demands rigid accuracy, not literary skill.

Construing and translation. 229

Translation divides itself naturally into two kinds; first, Translation from another language into English; secondly, Translation from English into another language, whether in prose or verse.

A strong and well-defined distinction ought to be drawn between Translation and Construing, though there is much in common. A Translator has to show that he is master of the two languages he is dealing with, and not a learner of one only; and that he can on principle render the one into the other as a first-rate modern writer would write it, giving intentionally and consciously the exact counterpart in each instance, however different the actual words or constructions may be. No boy ought ever to be allowed to translate who cannot first construe. But a little translation should be done in every class of the School.

In Translation into English there are three main paths which can be intelligently followed by a master of language.

First, there are Parallel constructions; by which is meant all instances where one language invariably, or nearly invariably, employs one construction in a given sense, and another language another, e. g.,

Si comes exstincti manes sequerere mariti
Esset dux facti Laodamia tui.

If you followed—Perfect Indicative,

Laodamia would be–Perfect Conjunctive. These two constructions being in parallel use for the Imperfects, which never occur in English Literature.

Or again, xayw /jm0ovir IXij a,

And I heard and was silent.

230 Analogous, corresponding.

Versibus propositis, pronuntiabam, I selected lines, and spoke them. Secondly, there are Analogous expressions, e. g., "pares cum paribus," "birds of a feather." " dypiovs o"yas," " a wild-goose chase, and a number of words and expressions which grow out of different habits, e. g., " Secunda castra," " the second days march."

Thirdly, there are Corresponding expressions, as the use of adjectives and adverbs in English for compound prepositions in Greek or Latin, e. g.,

"r! js evvoias Sia/mpteiv, "to entirely lose."

"perdiscendum jus civile," "we must thoroughly learn."

The use of Substantives for Verbs, e. g.,

" Ovk aurxpov (os yvvaiid yivva. ia. Xakelv,"

"as well befits a noble ladys lips." " exaedificare," " finish the whole building." " Impulsa cupressus Euro," " beneath the stroke." "In sleep," "dormiens," in haste, etc., with all ex-pressions of this kind in English, which in Greek or Latin become participles or adjectives, are examples of this.

Nothing is more constant or more important than the frequent use of the strong substantive in English for the strong verb in Greek or Latin.

Again Moods and Tenses in Greek and Latin must frequently be rendered by an adjective, adverb, or periphrasis, in English, e. g.,

C, he continued sending, or, he ofcen sent,

Counterparts. 231 or, he sent many, or, he sent at that time, e, he tried to prevent. The context must decide in each instance what the rendering must be. And both Teacher and learner must remember that there are some moods, and tenses, the latter especially, which are never found in English in the mood and tense shape. But these few hints will have shown that a master of language has a perfectly sure and scientific system to go by, and is quite at home in these variations. A good Translation is not a matter of happy chance, but however beautiful it may be proceeds by well-known laws. The best translation is the most complete rendering of the sense into simple and perfect English with the least possible change. A good translation is the most complete rendering of the sense into simple, and perfect English, without contradicting any idiom of Tense, or Mood, in the original.

Lastly, there are varieties of arrangement and sentence shape, which may be called Counterparts in language: as in English the omission of many connecting particles, where the more exact Greek or Latin puts them; the putting in many connecting particles, where Greek and Latin use tenses, relatives, etc.; the breaking up the long

Greek or Latin sentence into short sentences for the same reason. All these and like changes the intelligent Translator, who is master of both languages, observes intentionally; an unintelligent Translator does occasionally by habit. It is well to remember that a sentence, which is perfectly correct and idiomatic if used on " IoTiguage at all, if its structure is 232 The learners object.

continued ten times following, because another language continues it ten times following.

Every good Translator will take the thought of the passage, disconnect it from the grammatical structure, and try how a first-rate writer would put the thought. This will very often give the true rendering, and preserve all the sense in such a way as to show clearly that the Translator knows the structure, though he has not followed it.

In school work it is well to remember that the learners first object in an examination is to show his knowledge of Greek, or Latin; therefore in translating out of those languages into English, if he is obliged to sacrifice anything he must sacrifice the English, rather than fail to show that he is master of the Greek.

Notes taken in school should be very sparingly allowed; a note book is not attention, neither is it a boys mind.

A few words on Translating from English into Latin or Greek may be useful.

First, if the learner has really been in the habit of Translating Greek and Latin, then the English words will suggest and remind him of the Greek and Latin words for which he has used them. If he has only construed, or he has never used the words found in English literature, excepting by accident, he will have no words to remind him of Greek or Latin.

In Composition, intelligent thought is the object aimed at.

Most mistakes in rendering from English into another language arise from having no real understanding of the English.

How to translate. 233

Boys make their efforts a foolish struggle with words. What word can I get? not– what is the best way of putting the sense? is their starting point. This leads to nothing. Thoughtful understanding the sense is the true start. A boy is first required to show he is not a fool, a very different thing from whining out that he is not a poet.

Intelligent thought is shown first, by a thorough mastery of the true sense and spirit of the passage. It is a good practice to learn by heart the passage to be translated. A Teacher will point out shades of meaning, the appropriateness of epithets, the proportion of the ideas, and all other things which go to make a passage an harmonious whole, according as these requirements are violated by mistakes.

Diction and Vocabulary are got by thinking of English synonyms, and putting the sentence into different shapes.

True work is done not by hunting for words, and torturing them into place, but by changing the structure, e. g., by turning the subject into the predicate; the epithets into subjects; object into subject; substantives, adjectives, and adverbs, into the relative clauses, which they really are; and framing rapidly new combinations when one will not do, e. g., "Tis a merry world," the world smiles with merriment, with pleasure, with sweet hope, with delight, etc. Delight rules the world, people, hearts, etc. Hearts glow with joy, etc. A complete mastery of the sense does the work.

The genius of languages should be pointed out, e. g., the tendency of Lati verbs, tenses, 234 The requirements of Composition.

and moods, because the language expresses them gracefully; the tendency of English to suppress them, or use substantives, adjectives, or adverbs, in their place, because the English language has no graceful forms in this direction. In fact, all work is determined by the tools; a man with a chisel, and a man with an axe, will produce different works of art.

Remember, that the object of a Translator into English is in the first instance to show his knowledge of the language he is translating, therefore if anything must be sacrificed he must sacrifice elegance to accuracy. Whilst the object of a Translator into Latin or Greek is to show his knowledge of the language he is translating into, therefore he must sacrifice accurate rendering to elegance, if he must sacrifice.

The use of books of Composition is noxious. Each master ought to cook the exercise according to the digestion of his class, and not serve out regulation rations of salt beef to invalids. Then also he knows what to do in looking over the exercises, and what he has a right to expect from the boys.

Every third exercise, all through the school, ought to be original. That is, either a subject given, or ideas on a subject suggested, more or less fully, according to the capacity of the class.

Every subject ought to be carefully selected.

First of all, there should be certainty that the boys know all about it Secondly, it should be attractive as far as possible.

Hence, no subject in morals, or abstract questions, or ancient, unfamiliar persons or scenes, ought ever to be set.

How not to do it. 235

A short story, a description of some familiar fact, or scene, is the proper style of subject. Proverbs sometimes furnish good subjects. An episode in an interesting story which they can read, to be enlarged and composed afresh, is a good form of suggesting ideas to a class.

Original Composition means the rousing observation, the giving the seeing eye, and training the mind to make an harmonious picture out of what it sees, so that others may know it. Original Composition demands that such striking points shall be seized as mark out the thing spoken of in a peculiar and special way.

No boy ought ever to be allowed to tell you that stone is hard, rain wet, and the sun hot.

No boy ought ever to be allowed to tell you an auctioneers catalogue of dry facts, one after another; as, " summer ending tells of winter coming," etc.

No boy ought ever to be allowed to put a big lie, as–" there are no flies, every bird is silent, all the trees have lost their leaves, etc.;" when, as a fact, every tree is in a different stage of leaflessness, rooks caw, flies climb up the window pane, and so on.

No boy ought even to be allowed to tell a lumping truth. "Fifty thousand men were killed." Who cares? but tell how one died in a natural touching way, and every eye shall be wet with tears. This shows what true composition is, it is a fine perception of little truths expressed in a vivid way, and worked up so as to form an harmonious whole, with every part in its place.

Every picture must start from copying reality. A boy who goes into his study to evolve out of his inner consciousness a description of a hawthorn is as foolish as a 236 Language versus words.

painter would be who did the same. Genius is the power of getting inside a subject by loving it, not a power of flying above it.

In looking over Composition, remember, that an exercise full of word mistakes, which shows attention to teaching, and earnest effort to get out the thought and spirit, may be a very promising exercise, and an exercise without a fault in Grammar be most despairing. Thought comes first.

Every one can be taught to have the seeing eye, which is the beginning of all original composition. This has been shown in a former chapter.

It is a masters business to teach how to think. He must keep thought always before the minds of the Class as their object. He must show the boys how to see, giving them the seeing eye; first, for facts, as for the hare in the field, the structure in the plant; secondly, for the lessons in facts, their subtle truths, the life in what seems inanimate. Facts the food of thought, and thought, this first, this last. The seeing eye and the skilful tongue, able to express what is seen and felt, are his work. Teaching is infinite, for human nature is infinite, and human nature is its subject, and the highest thoughts of the highest minds in the noblest shapes are the instrument by which the teacher of language works.

The Thought determines the words, and in spite of the great difference in the natural powers of languages, and the genius of the speech employed by different races, there is, if the thought is studied, a sure and scientific way of treating every diversity that can arise–But a master of language is very different from an authority in words.

CHAPTER XII.

A Schoolboys Chapter.

Mind and life are the work you are engaged on. Lives, not lessons, your own lives, are the work, and the prize of work.

1. Throw away all idea of memory being your instrument, or knowledge your object.

Memory-knowledge, as such, is absolutely useless.

Memory-knowledge as training is worse than useless.

Memory-knowledge is often a disguise for mental incapacity.

Dead lumps of memory-work are dead.

A parrot is a parrot whether dressed in feathers or a coat.

2. Mind is known by what it puts out, Memory by what it casts in.

Mind is life. Live in your work. See the people, see the ground, see the scenes. If Scipio is named, see 238 Trollopes axiom.

him. Make in your mind a picture of Scipio, a person to represent the name; no matter how unlike the reality. The Dutch translator, who made "der Burgermeister Hannibal" drag cannon over the Alps, had a strong idea of what Hannibal was, and what he was about. The great painter, who painted Abraham leading his men against Chedorlaomer in the armour of an Italian soldier, had a strong idea of what Abraham was about. Trollope says in his wonderful Chapter on Novels and the art of writing them, in his Autobiography, " on the last day of each month recorded every person in the novel should be a month older than on the first" Here the whole science of how to work is summed up in a single sentence. Alas, there is no person at all in the Schoolboys Novel, in the work of his life. It is all hearing, no doing, no seeing, no picturing, no reality. If the best acting on the stage cannot ram reality into the mind how can a lesson you kick at? But as far as it is unreal it is nothing to you. You never forget a thing you do, cricket, for instance; or even the sitting in School. It is part of your life. But your book-work is not part of your life. Make it so. You cannot drop what hand, foot, eye, or brain, have really done, it is part of yourselves belonging to hand, foot, eye, or brain, but your book-work is shadow-work, a parrot-like struggle with words. Mere sound, that goes with the sound. Alter this.

It may help to alter this, if the stages are set down through which a fact can pass in the mind of a learner.

Take Hannibals passage of the Alps as told by Livy for the narrative you have to master and remember.

How to learn. 239

Now let us number roughly the mental possibilities.

i.–The fact catalogue, a mere exercise of memory.

2.–A useful idea of the facts.

3.–A mental picture of the scene, with all the facts and persons actually seen as in a picture. A real sketch, however slight, made by the learner for himself is a wonderful help.

4.–A thrilling and imaginative feeling for the picture, life breathed into it.

5.–A varying, and reconstructing, and enlarging, as a novel might do, the whole scene.

These five stages are the five main landmarks of mental progress in learning. The crossing the gulf between 2 and 3 marks decisively the passage from deadness to life. Anyone can begin though the highest never end. A child can see the vital distinction between writing out an invoice of the facts, like so many sacks of corn, even when it is done, and the degrees of mental skill represented by pictorial vividness, and thinking in shape.

The main rules of how to learn are simple.

i.–See. Then examine what you see; lastly, answer, or write.

2.–Make no attempt to remember anything you can put before your eye, or picture to your minds eye. Memory is not sight. For example:–What is an apple? The answer to this question ought to distinguish an apple from all other fruit. The question is one, the answer is manifold.

240 The mind and its pictures.

I.–Picture an apple. Put 4.–Note its colour.

one before your eye; 5.–inside, its texture.

really, if possible; if 6.–its parts, pips, core, not, picture it in your etc.

mind; see it there. 7.–its skin.

3.–Note its size. 8.–its juice.

3.–its shape. 9.–Compare with other fruits.

All these facts are seen, as soon as the apple is seen, and intelligent sight gives the answers to the question.

The untrained boy begins to try and remember what he knows about an apple, and flounders hopelessly for ever, though so familiar with the common thing, as he thinks it.

Next, let a picture be taken which has to be imagined in the mind. For example:–Describe a field as a study of colour. Select, and picture.

I.–Time of year–autumn. 6.–Bounded by hills on one 1.–Time of day–afternoon. side.

3.–Kind of day-Great clouds, 7.–Trees and hedges.

with sun. 8.–Water.

4.–Stubble. 9.–Cattle.

5.–Ground broken and un-10.–Aspect–south-west.

even.

When the mental eye has got this picture put together, the mere sight of the familiar objects will supply words and thoughts. Better still if the writer can go and see his field, and notice the variety of colour.

Next, let this be applied to the study of language. For example:–What is the construction of "quum"? or "when" in English?

"Quum" and "when" have two meanings.

Frame sentences to find this out. E. g.– i.–"When the end has come, the past is gone." 2.–"When I am at school, I play at cricket."

New words new thoughts, 241

Examine these two sentences, both of which speak of time, and both use the same word "when."

But here the likeness ends. "When" in the first sentence means the exact moment. "When" in the second sentence assuredly does not mean, even to the idolater, ever-lasting cricket; but cricket at various indeterminate times. In other words; the sight of two well-selected sentences, in which "when" occurs, reveals that either a particular moment or time is very positively meant; or any time in a longer period, it may be over thousands of years; two as entirely different thoughts as can enter the mind. The precise moment determines absolutely the use of the Fact Mood, or Indicative. Any moment determines absolutely the use of the Thought Mood, or Conjunctive.

Pictures in this way by sight give the reason first, and supply the rule afterwards, and fix both in the mind.

N. B.–Never comment on nothing. He who speaks before he has got a certainty before his eye, comments on nothing. Frame, or get an example. This is the law of all true work.

When out walking shut your eyes, and then picture to your mind the landscape before you. You will discover how little you have really seen.

When reading shut your eyes, and then picture to your mind the facts you are reading. You will discover how little you have really seen in what you read.

Every narrative in the world is composed on the same plan. The laws of narrative are simple, and can be laid down. These laws equally apply to the work of the composer, or the reader of the composition.

242 New words new thoughts.

1.–Note carefully every thing mentioned, or which comes into the field of description.

2.–Examine the inner meaning, the associations, the special powers of each thing per se.

3.–Note carefully the people, or creatures, mentioned.

4.–Examine the inner meaning, associations, and special life of each per se, 5.– Take the facts of the narrative: i. e. how things, or persons, or creatures, figure in the circumstances, which are narrated, or have to be narrated.

6.–The deductions and conclusions that may fairly be drawn from the narrative by a competent judge of all these facts.

All narrative composition proceeds on this plan; though a narrator does not necessarily deal with all the six heads, but selects according to his object in writing.

An illustration, and a sort of memoria technica, will make plain how a skilled workman treats his subject

Every school class is assembled in a class-room of some kind.

Let the class-room be the subject of the proposed composition, and an hours work with the class.

The skilled workman will first carefully note the room itself, its walls, its architecture, its size, the building it forms part of, its ceiling, its floor, its decoration and colour, or the absence of them; then, the furniture, the desks, the tables, the benches, the chairs, their variety or sameness, the fittings, or want of fittings, ornaments and illustrations, photographs, pictures, maps, models, wall-paintings, or the absence of them all.

Then he would consider the history of all these.

New words new thoughts. 243

For example, the building may carry the composer back through centuries of educational history, and must show the judgment passed by those who built it on education, or the means they had at their disposal.

Next comes the Class itself, the boys, the Master, and their private history as regards education, together with the work they are engaged on, their books, and order.

Then, and not till then, is a composer in possession of his material, and in a position to give a narrative of the morning lesson; when the construing or reading, the questions asked, the mistakes made, the gestures, attitudes, words, and behaviour, of each and all, would be passed in a spirited manner before the eye of the reader. And, lastly, when all this was done, the narrator himself, or a competent judge of his narrative, would be able to deduce with absolute certainty, as far as the narrative went, a complete history of the state of education, its merits, its defects, in the country where the narrative took place, to fix the time, comment on the time, and with great truth up to a certain point decide the position of that generation and people in matters of education.

All this is involved in one hours school-time in a class-room, where the untrained only see four walls, bare or decorated, a little furniture, some shabby books, too much ink, and twenty boys.

No rules can make you write a vivid narrative.

But a knowledge of these simple laws can show the most ignorant how to set about it with success.

It is impossible to translate nothing into something. Unless the English to be translated is thoroughly understood Aristotle himself would write nonsense.

244 Why we learn? Why not?

The unknown cannot teach the unknown. Unless your own language is known you can know nothing more well.

New words mean new powers of thought.

It is computed that an uneducated man uses 500 words. Shakespeare, it is said, has used 15,000. The Schoolboy who will not study words had better follow the plough, for he will never be a thinker of thoughts.

If you dont do small things youll never do great things.

Trifles are trifles to know, but not trifles to leave undone, or not to know.

Sitting over a book, and using your mind are not the same. Breeches-wear and brain-wear are not the same though the same time may be spent.

The humble fool does nothing he is told, calls himself stupid, and idles because of it.

The cross-grained fool abuses the masters as well.

The bumptious fool is an oracle on Education; and wishes to change everything he does not know; an extensive programme.

The reasons why we learn are simple.

i.–Skill is the object of all good work.

2.–Skill means the power of doing exactly what is wanted to be done, at the right time.

3.–Skill is produced by thought and practice.

4.–Anyone without skill is so far without education.

5.–Memory is not skill, and may be an hindrance to skill.

6.–Skill does not mean being full, but being master of strength, and trained movement.

Axioms and rules. 245 7.–The trained mind is worth all the knowledge in the world.

Why you do not learn.

i.–Because you suppose knowledge is all in all.

2.–Because you only half believe in knowledge.

3.–Because you dont think you shall get it.

4.–Because, if you get it, you dont quite see the use of it.

5.–Because the gain, if a gain, is so very far off.

6.–Because the present process is very unpleasant.

7.–Because it is certain that many cannot get much.

8.–Because great fools are sometimes seen full of knowledge, and great fools still.

9.–Besides other less creditable reasons.

But every one can get skill, and strength. Skill and strength are always pleasant, pleasant at the beginning, pleasant in the middle, pleasant at the end. Want of skill, and the ignorance which betokens want of skill, where there has been proper teaching, is not a misfortune, but a crime. Lives not lessons are the work.

Some Axioms and Rules for Learning.

i.–Do what you are told.

2.–Never guess.

3.–Nonsense never can be right.

4.–No one is obliged to be a fool because he is ignorant.

5.–Sense first, think, then write, or speak.

6.–Put what you know, as you know it.

7.–In translation never omit word, or syllable, particularly compounds.

8.–Never insert what is not there.

246 Some use for " never ".

g.–Never translate in defiance of the main sense, people, and actions, spoken of. Be ready to answer what the passage in hand is about.

10.–Never change the order of clauses, terms, or even words, without reason.

N. B.–A fool is a person who does not use the sense he has got.

Verses.

i.–Never put " tego " unless for a coverlet.

2.–Never put "ipse," "que," "en," "ecce," etc., to fill up a line.

3.–Never put "est" with a noun, or adjective, as an ordinary auxiliary verb.

4.–Never put "omne" for everything, or any adjectives without substantives, unless you can quote in support of your word.

5.–Never put stock phrases, "tempus in omne,;, "lata per arva," " tollit ad astra."

6.–Never end a pentameter with a short syllable.

7.–Never put epithets and their nouns together twice in the same sentence.

8.–Never put words together, which are not to be taken together, but can be. i i i i i i, as contrasted with 321231. In the first instance no one can know which figures pair together. In the second the pairs are seen at once.

Never be doing nothing. Either work, or play, or sleep. Never combine two of these.

These observations may appear truisms, or trivial, or unpractical. Try and work by them; they will vindicate their claim to be listened to.

CHAPTER XIII.

THE PRACTICE OF TEACHING.

Punishment.

The subject of punishment does not fall directly under teaching; yet it cannot entirely be left out, as it is one of the most difficult questions with which a school has to deal. But the author has treated of its main principles elsewhere.

If the school work is carefully adapted to the powers of the boys, and the boys themselves are all tested daily, it becomes a very serious puzzle how to punish satisfactorily the idle, the careless, or the undisciplined.

To punish by putting on more work, when the work already has been found too much, or, being enough, has been left undone, is absurd. Very little can be managed in that way, the wheels soon get clogged, and farther progress impossible.

education and School (Macmillan), Chapter XV.

248 Not punishment but improvement.

Whatever is done in the way of extra work ought to have an educational value, and keep in view the improvement of the boy punished

This axiom excludes all punishments in writing, unless given with a view to improve writing, or as a school exercise to be looked over, and corrected, like any other school exercise. But this looking over puts extra work on the master, who already has as much as he can fairly do.

Punishments which exact much additional work from the master are as impossible in a good school, as punishments which exact much additional labour from the boy. The true solution of the great difficulty appears to lie finally in a school having many privileges, as long as work and behaviour is good. Every privilege is a possible punishment, as it can be taken away. This is sometimes a severe infliction. Practically, there are two great hindrances to this expedient. Education is not sufficiently advanced to admit of a large number of privileges. They would be abused. And also the deprivation often lacks the one chief need in punishing, it is not quick enough.

Quickness and certainty soon reduce the numbers of faults. Uncertainty and delay breed culprits. But something can be done. If bad marks carry punishment, good marks should cancel it. The being in the first class should carry exemption from punishment, and require that the first offence should be visited by being turned out of sanctuary.

Again, if the size of the classes, and the working powers of the school, admit of individual cases being

Judicious blindness and deafness. 249 judged, and consideration shown without suspicion of favouritism, not what the fault deserves, but what will work best is the teachers problem. Many times a wise forgiveness has cured, where punishment would have made worse. The overmatched man and the fool have their punishments all cut-and-dried, of the regulation pattern, and apply the official stamp without regard to anything but the actual fault.

If work is set, then the demanding a certain number of lines of English or classical poetry to be learnt by heart is almost the only thing that cannot be evaded. But it is hard to be exact, and takes up much time.

The making a boy prepare the coming lessons, not the past ones, with more care, either by requiring a portion to be carefully translated, or in other ways, is sometimes practicable.

Somewhat in the same direction is the requiring a culprit, who has been guilty of a wrong construction in a sentence, to produce a certain number of examples of the right one out of the books he is reading.

The skeleton maps, which can be procured, may be utilised as punishments, by ordering the delinquent to fill in carefully a certain number of the names. A few lines of English verse on a subject, or a short narrative, or description in English, is a good form of punishment.

A little judicious blindness and deafness is a great J virtue in a wise teacher. As Solomon says, "Take no heed unto all words that are spoken, lest thou hear thy servant curse thee." The servant does not always mean it, and a man working on a plan will know when to tighten, and when to relax his grasp; when to see, and 2 5 What you command, obey.

when not to see. A dead level of punishment is a grievous mistake. It leads boys to think that however much they try there is no escape, and accordingly they lose heart, and cease to try. Glimmerings of better things should be taken advantage of, and when honest praise can be awarded the battle is half won.

Matters sometimes come to a crisis with a boy, and he feels it, and knows that the master has right on his side. He is both afraid, and ashamed of his misdeeds: a kind talk, a free pardon, and a fresh start, is sometimes very effective under such circumstances.

Choose what to punish carefully. It is a grievous mistake to allow boys to go on, and on, and on, with partial checks, until patience is exhausted, and then to break out on the next offender. Above all never inflict a punishment beyond what the evidence will prove, because a boy deserves it. If he does deserve it, be sure he will not be long before he gives the opportunity of letting him have his deserts without any possibility of his posing as a martyr. He will end the series by a notable act, which will be notable and plain, both to his own conscience, and to those important jurymen, his companions. Even lying excuses are often to be respected if they enable the speaker to deceive himself or his companions. It is better often to wait, and meet the boy on his own ground, and from his own point of view later on, for a later on will come, if the excuses are lying, when the guilt will be plain, and repentance possible. What you command obey yourself most. Perhaps there is no more unsuspected source of misdeeds than the unconscious way in which many masters break small laws, and

Masters and their copies. 2 51 disregard small observances. How often unpunctuality is fostered by a want of precision in the attendance of a master. Or his absence on some school occasion suggests that such public occasions are not worth coming to for their own sake, but are things to escape from if possible.

The boys extend the principle to things they wish to escape from; and no one suspects, least of all the delinquent master, that the heavy case of shirking which is tormenting him in his class is only an humble, but too successful copy of himself.

The attitude of masters ought not to be slovenly. The careless or sleepy posture reproduces itself in disagreeable ways. The true organiser, and sagacious trainer, will not cause disorder by standing in the way of a stream of boys, or, by coming in at wrong times, when numbers are going out. Boys are particularly alive to this kind of disrespect. Another grave cause of evil is the dishonour shown to the place in which the work is done. Things are allowed to be left about, and not put away when finished with, great roughness is permitted in the treatment of the room, and its furniture. Yet there is no law more absolutely certain than that mean treatment produces mean ideas; and whatever men honour they give honour to outwardly. It is a grievous wrong not to show honour to lessons, and the place where lessons are given.

The public opinion of any Society can expel any fault it pleases from that Society.

The public opinion of a school Society is formed far more by the private habits and character of the masters than the masters are at all aware of, or sometimes would 252 Only thieves have thieves honour.

like to be aware of. The authorities also should endeavour to form a healthy public opinion by making it pay, to use a slang expression, to keep the society clear of certain offences. As in many schools some reward is given when high Honours are gained, though the mass of boys did not gain them, so the mass may be made responsible, if wise conditions are laid down, for the dishonour and treason of a member of the school, though personally they had nothing to do with the actual crime. There is no reason in a true school, where true measures for giving each boy a thorough chance of doing his best are taken, why the old idolatry of "thieves honour" should exist. There is no more necessity in the nature of things why a school-boy, if given fair play, should protect and uphold cheating, lying, and evil in his companions, than why he should help a thief to escape in Regent Street.

By all means if the boys are thieves, and the masters are police, let the thieves stick to the thieves. But if boys and masters are united in an earnest, kindly struggle for good; and all the structure of the place, and all the habits, and all the currents of life show this; then down with the traitors and the thieves, who make themselves unworthy of trust and liberty, in a place framed for liberty, and worthy in all respects of trust, and allegiance. It is quite true that all this is a matter of much organization and care, and depends on questions of structure and detail, which are outside the present discussion; but it is also true that it is possible to get rid of "honour amongst thieves," and to make the school-boy see that unless he is a thief, which he has no business to be, the

Small barriers great safeguards. 253 old superstition must retire into the limbo of past follies, and be seen no more.

The main question of the principles, and even the practice of punishment, has been left very much untouched, partly because the author has written on it at some length in another book, partly because in a dissertation on Teaching what ought to be done to teach, rather than the means of grappling with non-teaching and non-learning, is the question; and punishment is but a by-issue. But it will be observed that much stress is laid on unobtrusively cutting off occasions of evil, preventing it, or meeting it at a very early stage. Small barriers are great safeguards. Small barriers wisely placed, and faithfully kept to, mark the sagacious ruler. The sagacious ruler is a perfect master of detail, not its slave; a master of detail, with his eye fixed on every first point of orderly training, most strict himself, and gradually getting others to be strict; but genial, and forbearing, dealing gently with the habits of a disorderly time.

As long as human nature is human nature, and learning to think a labour, and order opposed to the untrained boyishness, punishments will be needed; and needed in proportion to the difficulties under which the work is carried on. The ablest man overmatched in numbers, with all things round him dislocated and imperfect, must punish.

There are a thousand hindrances to the best work being done. As long as this is the case much preventable evil must go on. But in the abstract a single sentence liberally interpreted closes the whole question, "Honour the work, and the work will honour you."

Education and School (Macmillan), Chap. xv.

CHAPTER XIV.

CONCLUSION.

The dead hand, and the shadow of death.

Teaching is not a mere matter of competency or incompetency in the teacher. Unfortunately when all has been said, the conditions under which the work has to be done do affect the possibility of doing the work.

A school is a very complex structure. It is a mechanism of a very costly description; both the permanent outlay in buildings, and the annual cost of working, are great, and the requirements exceedingly varied. The buildings and grounds alone necessary for anything like thoroughly efficient work in a first-class school for 300 boys cannot be put at less than from,80,000 to; ioo, ooo, and upwards. Unfortunately also it is not possible to treat a school as a factory. Education is a

Trusts and Schools. 255 matter of dealing with life. And life will not stand still; so even if perfection is at the present moment reached, the perfection of to-day will not be the perfection of to-morrow; and if the movement of life is not allowed for, the life will either die out, or betake itself elsewhere.

In many instances the buildings and main funds of the school are furnished by what are rightly called Foundations. Thus a large amount of property exists for school purposes on the one hand; and all the school work is done by men who are not the owners of this property on the other.

There have therefore been in existence for many years, indeed from the beginning, two bodies of men in each school, the men in charge of the property, and the men in charge of the work.

Some thirty years ago before the nation woke up, and stretched itself, there was no system and much waste. In many instances the property had left the school, and the school had dwindled or perished, or the school had left the property in a great degree, and struck out a new line in freedom. Every one was doing what was right in his own eyes within certain traditional limits. Trusts and Schools, and Schools and Trusts, were in every conceivable state of undefined relation and anarchy. If that could be called anarchy where each went their separate way, that is, when there was an each in the case. For sometimes the Trust had swallowed up the funds, and sometimes a sinecure had done the same.

There was however one redeeming point in this state 256 Stir, criticism, hope.

of things of no mean significance. Like the Parochial life of England, however much that life may languish, there was nothing to prevent the life, if strong, from putting forth all its strength and creating a great school, or a most efficient system of teaching. There was also nothing to prevent the high hope in a workers heart that the truest form of life might push forth from within, grow, spread, and prevail, and that successful skill, and earnest experience, might bring order out of this unsettled material, and reform schools by presenting a better type as a model. Gradually the air became charged with that electricity of change, which, no one knows how or why, ushers in a period of movement, and, if it is but the tossing of a sick bed, compels some activity. Many minds were full of thoughts; many lips unsparing in criticism; hopes and fears according to mens tempers sprang into existence on all sides. Go where you might, talk of wasted endowments, of the dead hand, and neglected work, of useless trusts, and boys uneducated, and funds misapplied, or worse, was heard on all sides from every lip. The impossibility of true education was the universal theme, so long as schools were at the mercy of hands that felt not handling above, and the good or bad worker stumbling on below. The heart of England seemed to be stirred. A host of undefined longings, and fresh, keen hopes, and tremulous expectations, swept like a breeze through the land, and rolled the mists of stagnant places away. Every worker, whose heart was in his work, looked up, and thought winter was over, and spring was coming, and that living work would find freedom to grow. The dead hand was to be taken off.

The dead hand that is dead. 257

Trusts were no longer to weigh down schools, the skilled workman was to have fair play; Bumbledom and King Log were to come to an end, and a new era of enlightened liberty to begin. But what came of it all?

Much was heard of the dead hand; a captivating phrase, well-devised, and skilful; reflecting great credit on its inventors. There is much in a phrase. When once current, no one examines its meaning; a good phrase is worth ten thousand arguments. How often has a name carried all before it. There is a dead hand without doubt. They know it, who in their dark hour have felt it at their throat. They know it, who toiling in dangerous ways, have had its cold, hard grip pulling them back into ruin. But the hand of the dead is a very different thing from the dead hand. There is a dead hand without doubt, the pitiless hand of ignorant power meddling with life; which does not mean to be pitiless, but is pitiless, because it is dead; and being dead is thrust into living, palpitating life. But the dead hand is not the hand of the dead. The hands of the dead are oftentimes full of life, living powers in the kingdom of life. Those hands are not dead, those hands stretched out from the grave so full of ministering power. Those hands that night and morning have not failed to pass on the beneficent counsel of the wise head, the warm enthusiasm of the noble heart, the love that cast self aside, and gave in a free spirit in order to kindle the lamp of light and life for aftertime. Nay, they are not dead. Shall it be lawful in this wise modern world, and meet with complete immunity, lawful for hands to amass wealth, or inherit it, and then abuse it to every carnal lust, and every foul 258 Tlte hands of the dead that live.

indulgence of passion or pride, without hindrance; and not lawful to dedicate self and wealth to make your brethren of the same race better as the years pass on? Not lawful–so far that the law may not at any time step in, and claim as public property, because virtue has devoted it to a good end, the liberal bounty, that vice would have put out of reach by wasting it. Is the hand dead that gives its best to aftertime instead of sinking it in the all-selfish sea? And is the hand alive which takes the gift, not sparing always even living donors, and cares not for him who gave?

Let there be no misconception in this. If the end proposed by the giver is not good, destroy it. If it is extinct, replace it, change, modify, reassign. But if the giver gave a gift for a good end, and the main purpose of the liberal hand can be read with ease, as it generally can be, and can be translated into modern use, then the same immunity from confiscation, which the profligate secures by his vile spending on self, should be secured to him, who in his generous heart has spent on others. Is it true that the great purpose dies? Those hands are not dead, those living hands so full of ministering life, that never, from the first hour that the living heart brought forth its birth, have ceased their bounty, or wanted sons of light and life to receive it, and pass it on. It is a grand thing to know, for him who has the heart to know it, that the bread has been eaten,–bread out of hallowed hands, hands of the dead, so be it, hands hallowed by death, which has left only the glory and the goodness, the evil perished with the flesh,–that the bread as been eaten, century after century, by a brotherhood,

King Henry s bread. 259 each in his place, consciously or unconsciously, fulfilling his course, however much traitors may have been at work to betray; and some there are who know it. Some there are who count it a gracious thing, a holy debt, a gracious thing, and a high, to have eaten King Henrys bread, and received light and life from King Henrys hand. Who feel a soldiers allegiance in being of his band, in having the Kings most kingly chapel of Kings College their own, part of their inheritance, life of their life. Some there are, who go forth to their own life-work with the holy hand of the dead who live laid on their hearts, who feel that they have a debt to repay, who see a ray of life from afar cast upon all they do, and bear about for ever a light within, which they must pass on for the sake of the dead that live. If this be death, and the dead hand, how great should be the life that is to supplant it. And in a humbler way, though not less true, how many a quiet worker, standing in some ancient home of learning, about to begin, keen with fresh hope, and untried strength, and plans ready, before he enters on his lifes task has knelt in spirit to receive from the hands of the dead that live the half-fulfilled purpose of days of old as his inheritance to carry on; and has felt in the worst hour of after-trial the calm assurance of being one of the links of life; felt it a cause worth any overthrow; felt that he worked on holy ground, because of the man who in old time poured his life and blessing there, because of the seed sown in centuries past, and the harvest to be looked for in centuries to come. It ennobles the meanest to feel that they are part of a great living organism of life passing on life from the hands of the 260 Hope sprung to life.

dead that live, instead of being a screw in a Government machine, or the mainstay of a joint stock companys shares; honest positions enough, and capable of good, honest work, which good men and true can do, who deserve every honour they can get, but not the glow of a noble Hfe, not the power passed on by hands that live though dead. If this be the dead hand, then welcome death. But the hands of the dead filled England with life, and light, and hope.

No doubt an old house that has not been swept needs sweeping, but pulling down is not sweeping. It may need additions, and fresh arrangement, but pulling down is not addition. A time of awaking came over the land, and a very necessary inquiry took place. There was much that needed change when the awaking began, change in antiquated law, change also in the wakers up, change in the ways of blind custom, and funds misapplied, change in the hands that held, not change in the hands that gave, as far as their intention went, not scorn cast on the liberal hearts of old. All were agreed that the weight was to be taken off work; and the workers hearts beat high. It was a memorable time to those, who were at work; a time of promise, a veritable new world. The property of endowments was no longer to be the dominant power for good or evil, but the Schools and the work were to be all in all. The boys were to be taught, all of them, and no waste of the living material permitted any more. A standard of true work was to be set up, the principles of school with regard to cost and efficiency made plain, shortcomings exposed, and neglect and sham glory equally put to shame. These, and a

Hope strangled. Shadow of death. 261 thousand like dreams were dreamed according to the special views of the dreamers; but no one had the slightest doubt but that there was to be a breaking of chains, a letting of skilled workmen out of prison, an age of freedom, freedom in work, free progress, enlightened construction of schools, a starting point given for moving life in the present, and growth in skill, and a power of developing better methods provided for in the future.

The working world with its experience, its hopes, and its life, was soon taught how much better non-workers could manage their experiences, their hopes, and their life, than they could themselves. They learnt the meaning of the dead hand, when amateur power seized on the living organism of skilled work, stuck it on the official pin, made a specimen of it, and ticketed it in its own glass case. The Schools were tacked on as appendages to Trusts; and the skilled workman, engaged in the highest kind of skilled work, deliberately and securely put under amateurs in perpetuity. This closes the scene. Everything must lie in the shadow of this death.

Next the schools were tacked on to Examiners; who come fresh from their books to judge the work of the practical worker with all its varying factors, award praise and blame in total ignorance of those varying factors, and report this to the amateur power above, which knows still less. Even in the bookwork the process is misleading. Any original kind of teaching; any real advance, that is, or change of old methods is absolutely outside the examiners tether; any original kind of teaching, and 262 The dead hand, the shadow of death.

real advance in method, is accordingly killed at once under the shadow of this death. The dead hand is heavy on it. It cannot live.

Lastly, the simple question, what is necessary to enable a school to teach each boy, has neither been asked, nor answered. But if each boy is not really taught, then as far as the boys who are not taught and not trained are concerned, the school is no school. And as far as the masters are concerned, teaching in its true sense is impossible. This is death to the ordinary teaching. Hope is quenched. The shadow of death is over the land, and the dead hand on its teaching heart. If any seriously believe that the dead hand of external power can successfully deal with the most living, delicate, and progressive of works, true education, their armour is impenetrable by any words. And it is not the business of this treatise to enlarge on the subject.

Nothing that has been said in any way repudiates supervision, publicity, or a court of appeal.

The nation has a right to be assured that the endowments can do proper work, and are up to a fair level doing it. A pass inspection is honest for the teaching, and would not destroy life. The nation has a right to be assured that the funds are not misapplied, or made away with; a force of Trustees with a pass inspecting power for the School, and entrusted with the secular business, is competent to supervise the funds, and would not destroy life. But the present system does not necessarily enlighten the nation on these points, and is less and less likely to do so. Even if the system of vesting so much administrative power in non-working

The dead hand, the shadow of death. 263 hands was good in the abstract, the moment it has to be applied over a whole kingdom, and the wide area of national education, it must break down from the impossibility of finding a sufficient number of men competent from intellect, character, and position to exercise it.

It is a strange spectacle everywhere seen, though no one sees it; the spectacle of the nation putting their best hope, their children, under the charge of men whom they do not trust to do their work, and so put them in turn under the charge of others.

And those others enjoy the singular advantage of not knowing the work, and having neither opportunity, nor inclination to know it, with the additional recommendation of very often having been in earlier years hopelessly left behind by the very men, whom they now control in their own special profession and skill. But it is useless speaking on a subject foreclosed. The defeated get no hearing. The preachers of a lost cause are derided, till at some future time laws that tie up improvement, demands for what comes uppermost, impossible conditions of work, and the glorifying of unsound success avenge themselves on themselves; and all has to be done over again if there is health enough in the body politic; or if there is not, a worse thing follows.

How many hopes were raised, when the people woke up, which are now killed; hopes of liberty, free work, life, and living progress, which have all passed into the shadow of death, under the dead hand. How strangely the words of liberty sound. How are the swift feet prisoned in the Chinese shoe. The nation woke up. But there

264 Infallible power.

is an evil worse than sleep. Better to sleep, than awake, and make a noise about truth, and find truth troublesome and dangerous, and shut the door in her face, and sit down with all the self-satisfaction of the infallible, and rejoice,–with everything finished before anything is begun.

Caubkiugk: Jkinted By c. j. Clay, M. a. And Sons, At The University I-rbss

Euthyphro J. and A. M. Adam 4/6 i. 2/6
Protagoras Holden 4/6
Plutarch t. Demosthenes Gracchi :; 1
ii Nicias Sulla
Sophocles n Timoleon Oedipus Tyrannus 6/-Jebb 4/6
Thucydides Book III Spratt 5/-
Book vii Holden j/-
Xenophon Agesilaus Hailstone 2/6
M Anabasis Vol. I. Text. Vol. II. Notes. Pretor 3/-.6
,, I, II ,, 4f-
n I, III, IV, V 2/-each
t, II, VI, VII Edwards 1/6 2/6 each
n III Cyropaedeia I, II (2 vols.) II 1/6 Holden 6/-
ii
n ni, IV, V 5/-
n
t VI, VII, VIII t 5/"
2i.9.97

THE PITT PRESS SERIES.

2. LATIN.

Author Work Editor
Caesar De Bello Gallico
Com. I, III, VI, vii I Peskett il-iiI, and VII
Price i/6 each 1/-each 3/- 1/6 1/6 3/- In the Press 6 1/6 3/ 3/6
2/6 iv-v
De Bello Gallico I ch. 1-29 Shuckburgh
De Bello Civili. Com. I Peskett ,, Com. ii I,,
Cicero Actio Prima in C. Verrem Cowie ,, De Amicitia Reid ,, De Senectute,,
Div. in Q. Caec. et Actio
Prima in C. Verrem Heitland and Cowie
Philippica Secunda Peskett
Pro Archia Poeta Reid ,, Balbo,, ,, Milone,,
Murena Heitland
Plancio Holden
Sulla Reid
Somnium Scipionis Pearman 2/-

Cornellus Nepos Miltiades, Themistocles, Aris- tides, Pausanias, Cimon Shuckburgh 1/6 ,, Hannibal, Cato, Atticus,, 1/6 ,, Lysander, Alcibiades, Thrasybu- lus, Conon, Dion, Iphicrates,

Chabrias 1/6

Horace Epistles. Bk I 2/6 ,, Odes and Epodes Gow 5/- ,, Odes. Books I, III,, 2/-each

Book II, IV,, j6each

Epodes T/6 livy Books iv, vi, ix, xxvii Stephenson 2/6 each v Whibley 1/6

XXI, XXII Dimsdale

Lucan Pharsalia. Bk I . De Bello Civili. Bk viI
Lucretius Book v
Ovid Fasti. Book vi
Metamorphoses, Bk I
Flautus Epidicus ,, Stichus ,, Trinummus
Quintus Curtius Alexander in India
Tacitus Agricola and Germania Stephenson 3/-
Hist. Bk i Davies 2/6
Terence Hautontimorumenos Gray 3/-
Vergil Aeneid i to XII Sidgwick 1/6 each
Bucolics 1/6
Georgics I, II, and III, IV 2/-each
Complete Works, Vol. I, Text 3/6
Vol. II, Notes 4/6 2/6 each Heitland and Haskins 1/6 Postgate 2/-
Duff 2/-
Sidgwick 1/6
Dowdall 1/6
Gray 3/-
Fennell 2/6
Gray In the Press
Heitland and Raven 3/6 THE PITT PRESS SERIES.
3. FRENCH.
Author Work Editor Pria
About Le Roi des Montagnes Ropes 2!-
Biart Quand jtais petit, Pt I Boelle l/-
n La Suite du Menteur Pt II ,, 1-
Corneille Masson l/-
Polyeucte Braunholtz l/-
De Bonnechose Lazare Hoche Colbeck /"
Bertrand du Guesclin Leathes 2!-
ii Part II (With Vocabulary),, 1/6
Del vigne Louis XI Eve !
Les Enfants dedouard
DHarleville Le Vieux Clibataire Masson 2/-
De Lamartine Jeanne darc Clapin and Ropes 1/6
La Canne de Jonc V" 1/6
De Vigny Eve
Erckmann-Chatrian La Guerre Clapin
Guizot Discours sur lhistoire de la
Rvolution dangleterre Eve 2/6
Lemerder Frdgonde et Brunehaut Masson 2/-
Mme de Stal Le Directoire Masson and Prothero 2/
Dix Annes dexil l-
Mrime Colomba Ropes /-
Mlcnelet Louis XI and Charles the Bold " 2/6

Molire Le Bourgeois Gentilhomme Lcole des Femmes Clapin Saintsbury 2/6
ii Les Prcieuses ridicules Braunholtz 2/-
(Abridged Edition) ii /-
Le Misanthrope 2/6
LAvare t, 1/6
Filou La Mtromanie Masson i/-
Ponsard Charlotte Corday Ropes 1.-
Racine Les Plaideurs Braunholtz !/-
,, (Abridged Edition) M /-
Sainte-Beuve M. Daru. (Causeries du
Lundi, Vol. ix) Masson /-
Salntlue Picciola Clapin l/
Scribe and Legouv Bataille de Dames Bull l/-
Scribe Le Verre deau Colbeck /-
Sdalne Le Philosophe sans le savoir Bull
Souvestre Un Philosophe sous les Toits Eve t l/-
Le Serf and Le Chevrier de Lorraine Ropes Le Serf (With Vocabulary)
Thierry Lettres sur lhistoire de
France (xm–xxiv) Masson and Prothero
Rcits des Temps Mrovin giens, i–ni Masson and Ropes
Vlllemaln Lascaris ou les Grecs du xv" Sicle Masson
Voltaire Histoire du Sicle de Louis
XIV, Pt i, Ch. i–xni Masson and Prothero Pt n, Ch. xiv–xxiv
Pt ni, Ch. xxv–end
Xayler de (La Jeune Sibrienne. Le) M
Malatre j Lpreux de la Cit daostej Masson 2/6 a/6 2/6 1/6 THE PITT PRESS SERIES.
Author
Benedlz
Freytag
Goethe
Grimm
Gutzkow
Hacklnder
Hauff Immennann
Klee
Kohlrausch
Lessing 4. GERMAN.
Work
Ballads on German History
Dr Wespe
Der Staat Friedrichs des
Grossen
German Dactylic Poetry
Knabenjahre (1749–1761)
Hermann und Dorothea

Iphigenie
Selected Tales
Zopfund Schwert
Der geheime Agent
Das Bild des Kaisers
Das Wirthshaus im Spessart
Die Karavane
Der Oberhof
Die deutschen Heldensagen
Das Jahr 1813
Minna von Barnhelm
Editor
Wagner
Breul
Wagner
Pria 3l- 3l-
Wagner and Cartmell 2!- 3/6
Breul Inthe Press
Rippmann 3/-
Wolstenholme 3/6
E. L. Milner Barry
Breul
Schlottmann and Carlmell
Schlottmann
Wagner
Wolstenholme 3l- 3l-3l-3l-3l-
Raumer
Klehl
Schiller
Uhland
Wolstenholme In the Press Breul 3I-
Sime 3/-
Wagner
Lessing ft Geliert Selected Fables
Mendelssohn Selected Letters
Der erste Kreuzzug Wagner 2/-
Culturgeschichtliche
Novellen Wolstenholme 3/-
Die Ganerben and Die Ge-
rechtigkeit Gottes 3/-
Wilhelm Teil Breul 1J6
,, (Abridged Edition) 1/6
Geschichte des dreissigjh- rigen Kriegs Book III. 3/-
Maria Stuart,, 3/6
Wallenstein I. (Lager and

Piccolomini),, 3/6
Wallenstein II. (Tod) 3/6
Ernst, Herzog von Schwaben Wolstenholme 3/6 THE PITT PRESS SERIES.
Author
Bacon
Cowley
Earle
Gray
Macaulay
Mayor
More
Milton
Lumby 3/-
West 3/6 and s/-
Lumby 4/-
West In the Press
Tovey In the Press
Innes 1/6 i/6 In the Press
Pope
Scott
Shakespeare
Shakespeare and
Sidney
Wallace
West
Carlos
Mill
Bartholomew
Robinson 5. ENGLISH.
Work Editor Price
History of the Reign of
King Henry VII
Essays
Essays
Microcosmographie
Poems
Lord Clive
Warren Hastings
William Pitt and Earl of Chatham
A Sketch of Ancient Philoso-
phy from Thales to Cicero 3/6
History of King Richard III Lumby 3/6
Utopia 3/6
Arcades and Comus Verity 3/-
Ode on the Nativity, LAlle-j,, gro, II Penserosoand Lycidas j "

Samson Agonistes, 2/6
Paradise Lost, Bks I, II
Bks III, IV
Bks V, VI
Bks VII, VIII
Bks IX, X
Bks XI, XII, 2/-
Essay on Criticism West 2l-
Marmion Masterman 2/6
Lady of the Lake,, 2/6
Lay of the last Minstrel Flather 2/-
Legend of Montrose Simpson 2/6
A Midsummer-Nights Dream Verity 1/6
Twelfth Night, 1/6
Julius Caesar, i/6
The Tempest, 1/6
King Lear, 1/6
Merchant of Venice, In the Press
Fletcher Two Noble Kinsmen Skeat 3/6
An Apologie for Poetrie Shuckburgh 3/-
Outlines of the Philosophy of Aristotle 4/6
Elements of English Grammar
English Grammar for Beginners
Short History of British India
Elementary Commercial Geography
Atlas of Commercial Geography If.
I
Church Catechism Explained
THE PITT PRESS SERIES.
6. EDUCATIONAL SCIENCE.
Author Work Editor
Colbeck Lectures on the Teaching of Modern Languages
Coinenlus Life and Educational Works Laurie
Three Lectures on the Practice of Education
Eve I. On Marking
Sidgwick II. On Stimulus , v,
ADbott III. On the teaching of Latin Verse Composition
Farrar General Aims of the Teacher) v,
Foole Form Management i
Locke Thoughts on Education Quick
Milton Tractate on Education Browning
Sidgwick On Stimulus

Thrlng Theory and Practice of Teaching
Price . tin 1/6 3/6
7. MATHEMATICS.
Ball Elementary Algebra 4/6
Euclid Books I–vi, xi, xi I Taylor 5/-
Books I–VI 4/-
Books I–IV 3/-
Also separately
Books I, and II; 1II, and iv; v, and vi; x1, and xi I 1/6 each ,, Solutions to Exercises in Taylors
Euclid W. W. Taylor 10/6
And separately
Solutions to Bks I–IV 6/-
Solutions to Books vi. XI 6/-
HobsonandjesrOp Elementary Plane Trigonometry 4/6
Loney
Smith, C.
Hale, G.
Elements of Statics and Dynamics
Part I. Elements of Statics ,, II. Elements of Dynamics
Solutions of Examples, Statics and Dynamics
Mechanics and Hydrostatics
Arithmetic for Schools, with or without answers
Part I. Chapters I–VIII. Elementary, with or without answers
Part II. Chapters IX–XX, with or without answers
Key to Smiths Arithmetic
3/6
London: C. J. CLAY And SONS,
CAMBRIDGE UNIVERSITY PRESS WAREHOUSE,
AVE MARIA LANE.
GLASGOW: 163, Argyle Stbeet.
6 (ttambtfoge Bible for
anti (Stolieges.
General Educes :
J. J. S. PEEOWNE, D. D., Bishop Of Wobcebteb,
A. F. KIBKPATBICK, D. D., Beoius Pbofessob Of Hebbbw.
Extra Fcap. 8vo. cloth, with Maps when required.
Book of Joshua. Bev. G. F. Macleab, D. D. 2s. (id.
Book of Judges. Bev. J. J. Lias, M. A. 3s. 6(2.
First Book of Samuel. Prof. Kibkpatbick, D. D. 3s. (/.
Second Book of Samuel. Prof. Kibkpatbick, D. D. 3s. 6(2.
First and Second Book of Kings. Prof. Lumby, D. D. 3s. 6(2. each.
Books of Ezra and KTehemlah. Prof. Byle, D. D. 4s. (jd.
Book of Job. Prof. Davidson, D. D. 5s.
Psalms. Book I. Prof. Kibkpatbick, D. D. 3s. 6d.

Psalms. Books II and m. Prof. Kibkpatbick, D. D. 3s. 6(2.
Book of Ecclesiastes. Very Bev. E. H. Plumptbe, D. D. 5s.
Book of Isaiah. Chaps. I. XXXIX. Bev. J. Skinneb, D. D. 4s.
Book of Jeremiah. Bev. A. W. Stbeane, D. D. is. (Id.
Book of Ezeklel Prof. Davidson, D. D. 6s.
Book of Hose:. Bev. T. K. Cheyne, M. A., D. D. 3s.
Books of Joel and Amos. Bev. S. B. Dbiveb, D. D. 3s. Gd.
Books of Obadlah and Jonah. Arch. Pebowne. 2s. 6(2.
Book of micah. Bev. T. K. Cheyne, M. A., D. D. Is. 6(2.
HTahum, Habakkuk and Zephaniah. Prof. Davidson, D. D. 3s.
Books of Haggai, Zechariah and Malachi. Arch. Pebowne . 3s.6(2.
Book of Malachi. Archdeacon Pebowne. Is.
First Book of Maccabees. Bev. W. Faibweatheb and
Bev. J. S. Black, LL. D. 3s. 6(2.
Gospel according to St Matthew. Bev. A. Cabb, M. A. 2s. (id.
Gospel according to St Mark. Bev. Q. F. Maclkab. d. d. 2s. 6(2.
Gospel ace. to St Luke. Very Bev. F. W. Fabbab, D. D. 4s. 6(2.
Gospel according to St John. Bev. A. Plummeb, D. D. 4s. 6d.
Acts of the Apostles. Prof. Lumby, D. D. 4s. 6(2.
Epistle to the Romans. Bev. H. G. (1. Moule, D. D. 3s. 6(2.
First and Second Corinthians. Bev. J. J. Lias, M. A. 2s. each.
Epistle to the Galatians. Bev. E. H. Pebowne, D. D. Is. 6(2.
Epistle to the Ephesians. Bev. H. C. G. Moule, D. D. 2s. 6(2.
Epistle to the Fhilippians. Bev. H. 0. G. Modle, D. D. 2s. 6(2.
Colosaians and Philemon. Bev. H. C. G. Moule, D. D. 2s.
Epistles to the Thessalonlans. Bev. G. G. Findlay, B. A. 2s.
Epistles to Timothy and Titus. Bev. A. E. humphbeys, M. A. 3s.
Epistle to the Hebrews. Very Bev. F. W. Fabbab, D. D. 3s. 6(2.
Epistle of St James. Very Bev. E. H. Plumptbe, D. D. Is. 6d.
St Peter and St Judo. Very Bev. E. H. Plumptbe, D. D. 2s. 6d.
Epistles of St John. Bev. A. Plummeb, D. D. 3s. 6(2.
Book of Revelation. Bev. W. H. Simcox, M. A. 3s.
Other Volumes Preparing.
LONDON: C. J. CLAY And SONS,
CAMBBIDGE UNIVEBSITT PBES3 WABEHOUSE,
AVE MABIA LANE.
Bible for
Now Beady. With Maps. Price Is. each volume.
Book of Joshua. Bev. J. 8. Black, LL. D.
Book of Judges. Bev. J. 8. Black, LL. D.
First Book of Samuel. Prof. Ktbkpatbick, D. D.
Second Book of Samuel. Prof. Kibkpatbick, D. D.
First Book of Kings. Prof. Lumbt, D. D.
Second Book of Kings. Prof. Lumby, D. D.
Ezra and Nehemiah. Prof. Byle, D. D. Nearly ready

Gospel according to St Matthew. Bev. A. Caku, M. A.
Gospel according to St Mark. Bev. G. F. Macleab, D. D.
Gospel according to St Luke. Very Bev. F. W. Fakbab, D. D.
Gospel according to St John. Bev. A. Plummeb, D. D.
Acts of the Apostles. Prof. Lumby, D. D.
Cambridge mfe Cestamwt for Retools anb olugcs
Genebal Editob: J. J. 8. PEBOWNE, D. D.
Gospel according to St Matthew. Bev. A. C. mir, M. A.
With 4 Maps. 4s. Gd. Gospel according to St Mark. Bev. G. F. Macleab, D. D.
With 3 Maps. 4s. Gd. Gospel according to St Luke. Very Bev. F. W. Fabbab.
With 4 Maps. 6s. Gospel according to St John. Bev. A. Plummeb, D. D.
With 4 Maps. 6s.
Acts of the Apostles. Prof. Lumby, D. D. 4 Maps. 6s.
First Epistle to the Corinthians. Bev. J. J. Lias, M. A. 3s.
Second Epistle to the Corinthians. Bev. J. J. Lias, M. A. 3s.
Epistle to the Hebrews. Very Bev. F. W. Fabbab, D. D. 3s. 6d.
Epistles of St John. Bev. A. Plummeb, D. D. 4s.
Genebal Editob : Prof. J. A. BOBINSON, D. D.
Epistle to the Philippians. Bev. H. C. G. Moule, D. D. 2s. 6 1.
Epistle of St James. Bev. A. Cabb, M. A. 2s. Gd.
Pastoral Epistles. Bev. J. H. Bebnaed, D. D. In Preparation
Book of Revelation. Bev. W. H. Simcox, M. A. 5s.

Sondon: C. J. CLAY And SONS,
CAMBBIDGE WABEHOUSE, AVE MABIA LANE.
lag(iofo: 263, ARGYLE STBEET.
TLiip)is: F. A. BBOCKHAUS. eib Sort: THE MACMILLAN CO.
Cambkidoe: Peimted By i. ft c. t. Clay, At The

Lightning Source UK Ltd.
Milton Keynes UK
10 March 2011

169051UK00001B/65/P

9 780217 806596